The Spanish Civil War has been called "the most heroic and pitiful story of this century." From 1936 to 1939, there were two Spains – the Loyalists, faithful to the Republican government in power, held part of the country; the Rebels, dominated by their army, held onto the rest. Backed by the military might of Germany and Italy, the Rebels overcame the Loyalist armies; their commander, General Franco, has been ruling Spain ever since. Through the words of the European dictators, foreign writers and journalists, and the Spaniards themselves, Hugh Purcell analyzes how this tragic war erupted and how it affected the Spanish people and the world outside.

For the European dictators watching from the wings, the Spanish Civil War was a dress rehearsal for World War Two. Adolf Hitler, Benito Mussolini and Josef Stalin shipped tons of ammunition, soldiers and aircraft into the battlefields of Spain. For the European left-wing parties, it was "the last great cause" – the defense of democracy against Fascism. It sparked the imaginations of writers like Ernest Hemingway, George Orwell and Arthur Koestler, who joined the Loyalists in their combat against Fascism. Their writings about the war have become classics of our time. For hundreds of thousands of ordinary Spaniards, the war was neither glorious nor heroic – it was a devastating civil war ending in imprisonment, exile or death. Illustrated with fifty photographs and maps, *The Spanish Civil War* is a fascinating study of one of the most complex episodes of the twentieth century.

*Frontispiece* A patrol of Republican troops surrenders to Nationalist soldiers

# The Spanish Civil War

HUGH PURCELL

WAYLAND PUBLISHERS · LONDON
G. P. PUTNAM'S SONS · NEW YORK

Copyright © 1973 by Wayland Publishers Ltd
101 Grays Inn Road, London, WC1

SBN (England): 85340 271 X
SBN (United States): 399-11238-3
Library of Congress Catalog Card Number: 73-81026

Set in 'Monophoto' Times and printed offset litho in Great Britain by
Page Bros (Norwich) Ltd, Norwich

# Contents

# The Illustrations

# *Terminology*

Those who supported the Republican government in Spain
during the Civil War were known as Republicans or Loyalists,
because they were loyal to the legal government. The ultra-
nationalist groups, who fought for the over-throw of the
government, were known as Nationalists or Rebels.

# Introduction

"LESS THAN twenty years ago, most of us thought of Spain – if we thought at all about a country so removed from the stream of the world's affairs – as Europe's most decorative monarchy and least productive soil, a country of bull fights and gypsies, a tradition of Don Quixote and the Inquisition. Today Spain . . . is a preview of the sort of world that Fascism would establish for us if we allowed ourselves to be beaten in this war (1)."

These words were written in 1943 by Tom Wintringham who, with forty thousand other men from France, Germany, Austria, Italy, Britain, America, Canada, Scandinavia, Russia and Eastern Europe, fought unavailingly to defend the government in the Spanish Civil War. Its fall, in 1939, brought to power General Francisco Franco who has ruled as a dictator ever since. However, not all the international volunteers fought for the government. A smattering of Frenchmen, Britishers, Russians and Americans supported the Rebel army under General Franco, along with about a hundred thousand conscripts and volunteers from Germany, Italy and Portugal. So the Spanish Civil War was really a Western war. It was fought by Western soldiers with Western arms and money for Western ideas – Fascism, Communism and democracy. It was, in effect, a dress-rehearsal for the Second World War. Indeed, in 1938, Captain Liddell-Hart, then Military Correspondent of *The Times*, wrote: "The Second Great War of the twentieth century began in July, 1936 . . . The direct assistance which Italy gave with aircraft, and the indirect assistance which Germany gave with warships . . . were the first operations of the present war. What has followed in that

*A dress rehearsal*

11

*Opposite* East European volunteers to the International Brigades reach the Spanish frontier town of Le Perthus

theatre, the Far East, and now in Central Europe, form the modern equivalent of the familiar phrase of manoeuvring for position before the main stroke is delivered (2)."

*The great cause*  For European politicians, soldiers and ordinary men and women in the 1930s, the Civil War in Spain was their battleground and cause. Many saw it as a simple confrontation between Fascism and democracy, between dictatorship and freedom.

The writer Arthur Koestler, who was kept by Franco's troops in a condemned cell waiting to be shot for over two months, called the war "the last twitch of Europe's dying conscience (3)." An American father wrote to his soldier son: "I am pleased you are fighting. It is better to die for a cause than to live your whole life without one (4)."

The famous writer, Ernest Hemingway, used a verse written by John Donne, the seventeenth century poet, to express his own feelings: "No man is an Iland, intire of it selfe; every man is a peece of the Continent, a part of the maine; if a Clod be washed away by the Sea, Europe is the lesse; . . . any mans death diminishes me, because I am involved in mankinde; And therefore never send to know for whom the bell tolls; it tolls for thee (5)."

*The Spanish tragedy*  The "piece of the Continent washed away" was Spain and nearly a million people died in an attempt to stop it being torn apart. Many Western countries were affected by the war, but the tragedy belonged to Spain alone. The war was fought with a savagery and passion from which Spain is only now recovering. Over a hundred thousand Spaniards were executed, either singly or collectively, by their fellow countrymen off the field of battle. Their crime was simply belonging to the "wrong" side. A French writer describes vividly how men were arrested by General Francisco Franco's armed gangs. It is a scene which must still be a recurring nightmare to many Spaniards. It happened "every day from lost villages, at the time when they came in from the fields. They set off on their last journey with their arms still full of the day's toil, leaving soup untouched on the table, and a woman, breathless, a minute too late at the garden wall, with a little bunch of belongings hastily twisted into a bright napkin: '*Adios: Recuerdos*' ['Farewell: All the best'] (6)."

# 1 The Approach to War

ALFONSO XIII, Spain's last Bourbon monarch, abdicated in 1931. The local elections of that year had shown that the people had strong anti-monarchist feelings. In fact, Alfonso's decision was really a desperate move to prevent his own overthrow. His abdication announcement was dignified: "Sunday's elections have shown me that I no longer enjoy the love of my people. I could easily find means to support my royal powers against all comers, but I am determined to have nothing to do with setting one of my countrymen against another in a fratricidal civil war (7)."

*Abdication of Alfonso XIII*

After the abdication, a republic was established, but the governments that came to power were weak and corrupt. Discontent in Spain grew stronger. Because of the dis-satis-faction and resentment, two extremist groups were able to win the people's support and oppose the government. In part, the Spanish Civil War broke out because these two groups, the Falange and the Anarchists, opposed the government from either side. Both groups refused to participate in legal political procedures. In the end, the gun was mightier than the ballot box.

*A republic set up*

The Falange was a fascist-type organization. The word Falange comes from the Latin "phalanx," meaning a line of battle. It was founded by José Antonio Primo de Rivera, a tall, handsome lawyer in his early thirties with dark, brilliant eyes and an engaging smile. His movement was partly based on the beliefs of his father, General Miguel Primo de Rivera. The General had been appointed by Alfonso XIII in 1923 to manage the government, and he had ruled like a dictator for seven years.

*The Falange*

13

José Antonio, like his father, despised political parties and believed in ruling through the army. His hero was Benito Mussolini (1883–1945), the founder of Italian fascism. As with other Fascist movements, the Falange attracted a lot of support from the upper and middle classes, and from powerful business-men. They approved of its calls for law and order and for a dictatorship run through the army. The Falange also became pro-German and intensely nationalistic. One leader shouted at a rally: "We are going to exalt national sentiment with insanity, with paroxysms, with whatever needs to be. I prefer a nation of lunatics (8)." A poem entitled "Face to the Sun" was a battle hymn of the Falange (9):

> *Face to the sun, wearing the tunic*
> *Which yesterday you embroidered,*
> *Death will find me, if it calls me*
> *And I do not see you again . . .*
> *Arise battalions and conquer –*
> *For Spain has begun to awaken.*
> *Spain – United! Spain – Great!*
> *Spain – Free! Spain – Arise!*

The Falange was even active in Spanish Morocco in Africa. The secret Falangist cry there was *"Cafe!"* – which meant *"Camaradas! Arriba Falange Española!"* ("Comrades! Arise for a Falangist Spain!") One person who was mystified by this cry was the innocent Spanish High Commissioner. When he heard it at an official banquet, he asked why the guests were demanding coffee when the fish was still on the table!

*Death of Primo de Rivera*

When the Falange was founded in 1934 it attracted 75,000 followers. During the first year of the war, 1936, the number of supporters grew to nearly one million. José Antonio was against violence, but the Republican government thought that he was a dangerous man, the leader of a million militant supporters. He was thrown into prison early in 1936 and sent for trial. He defended himself brilliantly at the trial but collapsed when the death sentence was pronounced. In November, he was shot.

*The Anarchists*

The Falange was committed to overthrowing the weak Republican government. It was typical of many Fascist-type movements that existed in Europe between the two World

14

*Opposite* King Alfonso XIII (*left*) with the newly appointed leader of his Cabinet, General Miguel Primo de Rivera

Wars. On the other hand, the Anarchist movement was rooted in the political philosophy of the nineteenth century. The Anarchists' prophet was a Russian named Mikhail Bakunin (1814–1876). His message was simple. He believed that it was morally evil for a state to have complete authority and to demand unquestioning obedience from the people. He wanted to destroy the state, and replace it with self-governing bodies, such as collective farms and town communes. Each self-governing unit would make voluntary pacts with the others. Bakunin felt that this kind of society would only arise after all the kings and priests had been done away with – strangled in each others' guts, as he put it.

In 1934, the Spanish Anarchists published their manifesto, which was based on Bakunin's political thinking (10):

"There is only one regime that can give the workers liberty, well-being and happiness, it is Libertarian Communism.

"Libertarian Communism is the organization of society without a state and without private property.

"The centres of organization . . . are the syndicate and the free municipality.

"Workers in factories . . . group together spontaneously in the syndicates.

"With the same spontaneity the inhabitants of the same locality join together in the municipality.

"Under Libertarian Communism, egoism is unknown: it is replaced by the broadest social love."

The Anarchists were so against all authority, that it is hard to see how they would establish any kind of society. One journalist explained the Anarchists' dilemma: "When Maurin [a Communist] said, 'We must have so and so put into jail . . . ,' he was not allowed to go further but was interrupted by cries of, 'No more jails! We want to get rid of jails.' And if he explained, 'I meant that we must send usurers and hangmen to jail . . . ,' the response was, 'Dictator! No more, no more! Down with Russia!' (11)"

The Anarchists' dream of setting up small, self-governing societies without any means to enforce the law may seem to us naïve and unrealistic. But we must remember that in Spain workers and peasants were probably less educated and more religious than their counterparts in other Western European countries. Amidst the poverty and hunger of the Spanish countryside, the Anarchist teachers were welcomed as saviours. Among people desperate for a faith, they replaced the priests who were generally disliked for their corruption.

The Anarchist movement became very powerful in the years before the Spanish Civil War. Its main strength lay in the C.N.T. (the *Confederación Nacional del Trabajo*). This was a united trade-union movement, with branches in each city and *pueblo* (village). About 1,500,000 Spanish workers were Anarchist in spirit in the 1930s, and the C.N.T. was able to use a powerful weapon against the government – the well planned and ruthlessly operated general strike. The Anarchists' political wing, founded in 1927, was named the F.I.A. (the *Federación Anarquista Ibérica*). It numbered about 200,000 and became the revolutionary vanguard of the movement. The F.I.A. tried to achieve its aims by assassination and sabotage.

The Anarchists' leading, and now legendary, man of violence was Buenaventura Durruti. He was a heavy-set, powerful man, with dark skin, black eyes and full of animal magnetism. To some he was a "thug" and "killer"; to others a hero with an "imperious head eclipsing all others, who laughed like a child and wept before the human tragedy (12)." For years he blew up bridges, set fire to trains and raided banks. He even tried to assassinate Alfonso XIII. After this failure, he fled to South America and later returned to Paris to set up a revolutionary book-shop. His own revolutionary zeal was infectious. During the Civil War he told a Russian journalist: "It is possible that only a hundred of us will survive but with that hundred we shall . . . beat Fascism and proclaim libertarian revolution . . . we shall show you, Bolsheviks, how to make a revolution (13)."

Durruti did not survive. He was killed during the siege of Madrid in 1936, ten days after the death of José Antonio Primo de Rivera. Durruti was also shot, probably by a fellow Anarchist. "It was an act of vengeance (14)," said his widow. Those who attended the funeral mourned not only the death of a great leader. As it turned out, they were mourning the death of pure

*The C.N.T.*

*Buenaventura Durruti*

17

The poverty of Spain: a slum district of Madrid, 1930

Anarchism. One man present at the funeral remembered: "The funeral took place in Barcelona. It was a dark, cloudy day, and Barcelona was given over to collective hysteria. People knelt in the streets as the cortège passed with its honour guard of Anarchists in battle-dress. They wept openly. Half a million people were gathered in the streets, and none were dry-eyed. For Barcelona, Durruti was a symbol of the triumph of the Anarchist idea, and it was almost beyond belief that he could be dead (15)."

The revolutionary nature of both Falange and Anarchists, and their increasing popularity, shows that there was far more wrong with Spain than just a succession of weak and corrupt governments. Because both organizations refused to support any government and did not even vote for the *Cortes* (the Spanish Parliament), war was brought nearer. But the main reasons for the downfall of Alfonso XIII and the outbreak of Civil War five years later were the irreconcilable quarrels among the Spanish people over three issues: the land, the Church and regional self-rule.

*Reasons for the Civil War*

19

*Opposite* The coffin of Buenaventura Durruti, the leading Anarchist, is carried through the streets of Barcelona by loyal Anarchist troops

In 1936, Spain had a population of twenty-four and a half million people. Nearly seventy per cent of them lived on the land, but very few owned any of it: "Spain is a country of hunger; mainly of sheer physical hunger, but also of hunger for land . . . Sixty-five per cent of the population holds 6·3 per cent of the land, while four per cent of the population holds sixty per cent (16)."

*Poverty-striken peasants*

This semi-feudal structure provided the underlying discontent which led to the Civil War. The vast majority of Spaniards who lived on the land were extremely poor, particularly in the centre and south (Castile and Andalusia). One eyewitness wrote: "The houses in the villages in the interior of Spain often consist of a single room. Anyone looking in at the door can see the whole household; an iron bedstead facing the door, two or three chairs and a bench, a few primitive cooking utensils hanging on the walls, and invariably a swarm of children and dogs, to say nothing of flies. The single door serves to light the room, to provide entry and exit for men and beasts, and to carry away the smoke. In 1932 there were still . . . large numbers of agricultural workers and their families who lived like troglodytes [cave-dwellers] in caves and pits dug out of the hillside (17)."

*Hired workers*

For the multitude of landless peasants, working conditions had changed little since Roman times. From autumn to spring, their only hope of finding work was on the very rich estates. Agents from the estates would visit the *pueblos* (villages) in order to sign on workmen. The *braceros* (workers) would assemble at dawn in the village square, as in a slave market, "dressed in a loose cotton jacket with sandals of hemp or esparto grass (18)." For those who were lucky enough to get work, the wage was about three pesetas ($7\frac{1}{2}$p; \$.18) a day.

The tragedy of Spanish agriculture was that it could have been very rich; owing to the varied climate and countryside, most of the world's crops could be grown in Spain. Before the Civil War, however, the selfishness of the wealthy landlords and the bad management of their estates made Spanish agriculture very poor. Only three per cent of the whole country was irrigated. In 1932, the Republican government did attempt some reforms. These included a slight rise in wages and the introduction of an

20

*Opposite* During Alfonso XIII's reign the government made some efforts to help the poor: the King and Queen attending a ceremony to bless housing for poor families of San Sebastian

eight hour day. One peasant commented: "Our wives were able to return home at five o'clock in the evening and prepare the meal, and also have time for sewing and seeing to the children's clothes. We were able to go to meetings of our organization and spend a little time gossiping in the street . . . (19)"

These reforms were never fully carried out. In any event, they were not nearly enough to solve Spain's agricultural problems. As the future Prime Minister Largo Caballero remarked, the new laws were but "an aspirin to cure appendicitis (20)." The terrible hunger for land still remained. A foreign journalist wrote: "The *yunteros* [peasants owning a pair of horses but no land] waited hopelessly for some land to plough and cultivate. The Communists' slogan, 'The land to the peasants,' and the Anarchists', 'The land to him who works it,' were terribly real in the starving countryside (21)." The same journalist summed up the misery: "Hunger, sun, civil guard, trachoma, priests, unemployment, flamenco singing (that Moorish famine-wail), flies, illiteracy, infant mortality, excessive natality, beggars, syphilis and again hunger; this was the panorama of the Spanish countryside (22)."

*Hunger for land*

In the 1930s, the Catholic Church in Spain was as medieval as the system of agriculture. Although the government had con-fiscated Church lands in the nineteenth century, the Catholic establishment was still enormously wealthy. The Jesuits, particularly, were reputed to be vastly rich, holding shares in everything from antique furniture to night clubs and cinemas. "Money is very Catholic" was a well-known proverb.

The Church was a worldly, politically committed institution

*The wealthy church*

which supported the parties of tradition and military rule. It spread its views not only from the pulpit but also from the classroom, for many teachers were priests and many schools were run by the Jesuits. The Church catechism of 1927 contained these lessons which were always taught in church schools (23):

"*Question:* What kind of sin is committed by one who votes for a liberal candidate?

"*Answer:* Generally a mortal sin.

"*Question:* Is it a sin for a Catholic to read a liberal newspaper?

"*Answer:* He may read the *Stock Exchange News.*"

The Encyclical of Pope Pius XI, *Quadragesimo Anno* (1931), was another favourite text. One foreign writer of this period summed up its teachings: "The duties of the worker are: to work, not to damage the employer's interests, never to have recourse to violence. The duties of the employer are: not to consider the worker a slave, encourage thrift and pay a fair wage (24)."

When General Franco made his bid for power, the Church supported his cause and donated great amounts of money. One reporter commented: "Among the big five banks . . . was the Banco Espiritu Santo, the Bank of the Holy Ghost, which largely helped finance Franco's insurrection (25)."

Many Spanish people did not approve of the Church's business and political interests. The first Prime Minister of the Second Republic, Manuel Azaña, declared in 1931 that "Spain had ceased to be Catholic (26)." It was estimated at the time that less than two-thirds of the population were practising Catholics, i.e. attended Mass and Confession. In fact, most Spaniards had not really "ceased to be Catholic," for religious belief was deeply engrained in the Spanish character. Indeed, this is one reason why ideological disputes were waged with such intensity and passion. But Spaniards were anti-clerical. As the Anarchists declared in 1936: "The Church would be very fine if only it could be without priests (27)."

*Hatred of the priests*     The priests were hated because of their corruption, hypocrisy and alliance with the rich and the powerful: "It offended Spanish notions of human dignity that a priest should put on

22

clean vestments for a rich man's funeral and wear his dirty one for a poor man's. It offended Spaniards' high valuation of human existence that women [nuns] should be shut away from the world and condemned to a life of sterility (28)."

With the support of many Spaniards, in 1931 Azaña closed down the Jesuit schools and forbade any Order to engage in commerce. Instead of obeying the teachings of the Church, many Spanish workers became Communists or Anarchists. But they did not give up their essentially religious outlook. Instead, they fused their political and religious beliefs. During one small revolt, for instance, workers carried posters that read: "Long live the Red Christ, for He is one of us!" And, "We are Communists. Our knives for anyone who touches Her! [a statue of the Virgin] (29)."

The third simmering grievance which the Republican government of 1931–1933 tried to solve was the issue of regional self-rule. Spain had been united into a single state in the sixteenth century. But there still remained two regions, Catalonia and the Basque Provinces, which took such pride in their own customs and traditions that they wanted more independence. Each region had its own distinct language and culture. Each had a flourishing economy.

Catalonia was the industrial giant of Spain. One journalist reported: "Spain is the impoverished agrarian tyrant while Catalonia is the rich industrial rebel . . . Catalonia accounts for about ten per cent of all Spanish agricultural production but for eighty-seven and a half per cent of industrial [production] (30)." The C.N.T. and the F.I.A., the Anarchists' trade union and political wing, were very strong among the industrial workers in Catalonia. Buenaventura Durruti, the leading Anarchist, organized street riots and demonstrations which finally persuaded Prime Minister Azaña to pass the Catalan Statute of 1932. This brought limited home rule to Catalonia. For a short while the *Esquerra* (Catalonia for the "left") Party was in power. The party's leader was Francisco Macia, or *El Avi* (The Grandfather). He died shortly after the home rule Statute

*Catalonia*

23

REGIONS AND PROVINCES OF SPAIN

was passed, which prompted one historian to call him "the only Spanish statesman of the twentieth century to have died a success (31)."

The home rule Statute did not really satisfy the Anarchists. They were committed to non-government, or, at least, to genuine self-government. They remained a thorn in the flesh of the *Generalitat* (the Catalan Parliament) throughout its short life.

*The Basques*   Unlike the anti-Church and anti-government Catalans, the Basques were loyal to Church and tradition. Their motto was: "For God and our old laws." By "old laws" the Basques meant self-rule. Their republic was proclaimed on 7th October, 1936, after the Civil War had begun. The Basque Republic was known as *Euzkadi* (after its language, *Euskera*). The statement of its leader, Don José Aguirre, shows once more the deep Catholicism of Spaniards: "I regard it of particular importance at this moment to state emphatically that we of the Basque country are all with you against Fascism, and that we are quite especially so because of our undeviating Christian and Catholic principles . . . Christ chose neither bayonet nor gun to win the world . . . just as Christ came from the people, we are with Him and with the people in this fight (32)."

During the 1930s, many Spaniards seriously feared that their nation might once again fall apart into a group of self-governing regions. This fear was particularly strong among the Falange and the army, who were both dedicated to unity and nationalism.

So by 1933 the Republican government had antagonized the *Failure of the* wealthy landowners by its limited land reform, embittered the *government* Church and churchgoers by reducing the power of the priests, and then infuriated the army by granting home rule to the Catalans and, soon, to the Basques. At the same time, these progressive measures had not gone nearly far enough to satisfy "the people of Spain." The question many people were asking themselves was: could any government hold the country together and keep itself in power once the opposing forces of reform and reaction had been unleashed? The Anarchists and the Falange obviously thought not – both groups were waiting outside the political arena for an inevitable revolution.

It is now time to look more closely at the first government of the Second Republic, which came to power after Alfonso XIII's abdication in 1931: "The tasks which awaited the young republic were enormous, and it did not prove equal to them. It was with extreme timidity and hesitation that the Republican government tackled the burning problems that faced it, stirring up the embers of a smouldering crater, so to speak, with a drawing room poker (33)."

The man responsible for tackling these "burning problems" *Manuel Azaña* was the Prime Minister, Manuel Azaña. Before 1931 he had been a writer and a teacher and had never been involved in politics. Unlike Primo de Rivera and Durruti, Azaña did not owe any part of his success to his looks. Indeed, his face was so ugly that he was known by his opponents as "the monster." His main weapon was a cold and sneering eloquence. A contemporary recalled: "I once asked him for the reason for his mania of wounding simply in order to wound, of never losing an opportunity to pour scorn on the opposition, and he replied, 'I do it because it amuses me.' I am sure this was correct (34)."

Azaña was a liberal, an atheist, and kept himself aloof from

Prime Minister Azaña (*right*) rides in state through the streets of Madrid

*Need for*
*Socialist*
*support*

the people. In fact, he was very much the middle-class intellectual. This also was the character of the Republican Party. It had to rely on an alliance with the Socialists to gain support from the common people. The Socialists themselves relied on the U.G.T. (*Unión General de Trabajadores*, or Socialist Trade Union), for their main support. The General Secretary of the U.G.T. was the Minister of Labour in the Republican government. He was Largo Caballero, an honest, hardworking union official. He had risen to his high position through his own efforts, so he was a model for many Spanish workers. That is, he was a model for the workers who belonged to the U.G.T. and had not been attracted to the larger and far more militant C.N.T. of the Anarchists. By 1936 the U.G.T. numbered one and a half million workers. This large number partly explains the very small size of the Communist Party, which only had 35,000 supporters.

Azaña's government fell in 1933. One reason was that Largo Caballero withdrew the Socialists' support. The Republicans, he said, were ignoring the true interests of the Spanish people. This again shows Azaña's dilemma – a moderately progressive policy mainly worsened Spain's ills.

Power now passed to the right-wing parties – the C.E.D.A. (*Confederación Españolo de Derechas Autónomas*, or Catholic Party) and the Radical Republicans. The trouble was that their leaders, Alejandro Lerroux and Gil Robles, were in the same predicament as Azaña, only the other way round. Their policy simply amounted to undoing Azaña's reforms, but did not go far enough to please their backers – the Church, army and Falange. On the other hand, it obviously antagonized their enemies – the Republican Left, Socialists, Anarchists and Communists. As a Socialist said in a radio speech: "Now it cannot be said in Spain as did Marx at the end of the Communist Manifesto that the proletariat has nothing to lose but its chains. Now it has things to lose: all the political and economic gains that it has won (35)."

*A new government formed*

Spain was now in a downward spiral of chaos and violence which would finally lead to war. After the government put down several strikes and uprisings with great savagery, the parties of the left were desperate enough to unite into a Popular Front. At the next election in February, 1936, the Popular Front won a narrow victory with 4,700,000 votes against 4,000,000 for their opponents.

*Victory of the Popular Front*

So once again a weak progressive government held the stage, but power had now passed to the wings. On the left were the Anarchists and Communists who gained more and more supporters among the disillusioned and poverty-stricken Spanish workers. On the right the army and Falange became increasingly militant. The embers had been stirred, and the smouldering volcano was about to erupt.

The five and a half years of the Second Republic had aggravated the three quarrels which had split Spain for the last century and a half: the quarrel between the Church and liberals, between landlord and peasant, and between local rights and strict central government. In the end, the Second Republic failed because none of its governments was strong enough to prevent power passing out of its hands to the militant forces on the left and right.

The uprising came from the right. Since 1932, a group of Generals had been plotting a rebellion against the Second Republic. They had the support of most of the army commanders and were in league with the Falange. They were also backed by two ultra-conservative parties, the Monarchists and Carlists, who were working for the return of the exiled King Alfonso XIII. Adolf Hitler and Benito Mussolini had also given their blessing to the revolt. After the Popular Front victory of 1936, the planned uprising needed only co-ordination of all the groups and an excuse to act.

*Murder of Calvo Sotelo*

The excuse came in July when Calvo Sotelo, a staunch Monarchist and Opposition leader in the *Cortes,* was murdered. The official police report described what happened after the assassins entered Sotelo's house at night and roused him from his sleep: "Señor Sotelo then went into the children's room, kissing each of them in turn as they slept . . . He then took leave of his wife in the hallway, promising to call her from the police station, 'unless,' he added, 'these gentlemen have come to blow my brains out.'" Soleto was put in a lorry and driven through the streets of Madrid. The report continued: "The truck reached the point where Ayala and Velazquez Streets cross, and here Victoriano Cuenca drew out a pistol and fired two shots at the back of Señor Sotelo's head so quickly that the other men in the truck had the impression that only one shot had been fired. The victim slipped down on the floor between the seats (36)."

*Death of General Sanjurjo*

Soon after this murder, the army commanders received secret orders from the Generals plotting the rebellion. They were instructed to begin the revolt against the government on the night of 17th July. The man who was to take command of the uprising was General Sanjurjo, who was living in Portugal at the time. A private aeroplane was to fly him from Portugal to Burgos in Spain. The pilot of the plane later recalled: "The General climbed into the aeroplane with heavy suitcases. I suggested discreetly that it might be better to travel light . . . I

*Opposite* General Franco, leader of the Spanish Nationalists, or Rebels, at the beginning of the Civil War

Men of the Spanish Foreign Legion on parade before embarking for Spain

was told, 'They are the General's uniforms. He cannot arrive in Burgos without his uniforms, and on the eve of his triumphal entry into Madrid.''' General Sanjurjo never arrived in Burgos. He had not heeded the pilot's warnings, and the plane crashed soon after take-off because of the heavy suitcases. "When the flames died down, there was only the twisted wreckage and the poor white bones of the General (37)."

*Franco begins his journey*

The man who replaced General Sanjurjo as the leader of the revolt was General Francisco Franco. Already regarded as a dangerous threat to Azaña, he had been exiled to the Canary Islands a few months earlier. During this fateful July, 1936, he journeyed from the Canaries to Spanish Morocco in Africa. There he took command of the Spanish Army of Africa and began the long journey to Spain, accompanied by his troops.

Strangely enough, Franco was ferried on the first stage of his

30

journey from the Canaries by an English adventurer, Hugh Pollard, and two English girls. Pollard was a friend of Douglas Jerrold, editor of the near-Fascist *English Review*. Jerrold heard from his contacts in Spain that a plane was needed to fly Franco out of the Canaries. As the story goes, Jerrold telephoned Hugh Pollard, because, as Jerrold himself wrote later, the job was Pollard's by rights, for he had experience of Moroccan, Mexican and Irish revolutions – and, of course, this meant war. And he knew Spanish.

"'Can you fly to Africa with two girls?' I [Jerrold] enquired and heard the reply:

"'Depends upon the girls.'

"'There's only one point I ought to mention,' I concluded. 'The aeroplane may be stolen when you get there. In that case you come back by boat.'

"'First class?'

"'Why not?'

"'Can do. Goodbye' (38)."

The 18th July, 1936, was a Saturday. In Madrid, nerves were on edge because of the daily heightening of tension between Popular Front supporters and those of the opposition. The urgent voice of the radio, broadcast over loudspeakers, did not help: "People of Spain! Keep tuned in! Keep tuned in! Do not turn your radios off! Reports are being circulated by traitors. Wild stories are causing fear and panic. The government will broadcast day and night – learn the truth from this station. Keep tuned in! Keep tuned in! (39)"

*Nerves on edge*

The following morning the first news of the Generals' revolt was broadcast over Madrid radio: "Attention! People of Spain! The rebellion against the Republic, led by a handful of traitorous generals, began with the Moorish troops. They persuaded their soldiers, by the use of the most vicious lies, to rise against the Republic . . .

*The uprising begins*

"In the meantime, other members of this conspiracy against liberty have incited isolated regiments in the north and south to rise against the Republic . . . Malaga has been attacked and is in flames. Government forces and rebels are fighting in the streets of Barcelona (40)." The Civil War had begun.

# 2 The Two Spains

THE GENERALS launched their uprising on 18th July, 1936. Three days later a rough dividing line could be drawn, separating the areas where the uprising had been successful from those where it had failed. Apart from the Basque Provinces, the north and west of Spain became Nationalist, or Rebel, territory. In these areas, the Generals had control. The south, east and north-east continued to support the government and remained Republican, or Loyalist. The Nationalists did, however, capture some isolated towns like Granada and Cordoba in Republican territory. Morocco, the Canaries and Balearic Islands (except Minorca) also went over to the Rebels.

During the first few months of the Civil War there were not just two Spains, but several hundred. Regional differences and bad communications split up the country into scores of distinct uprisings. Government officials in Madrid telephoned civil governors in different regions to learn what territory had been lost. They knew the government had been defeated when a Rebel commander answered the phone, shouting insultingly, "*Arriba España!*" ("Up with Spain!")

*Hundreds of Spains*

Some of the army officers who led uprisings against the government were daring men. The entire garrison at Seville was captured almost single-handed by General Gonzalo Queipo de Llano. He managed this extraordinary con-trick by entering the garrison headquarters on Saturday, 18th July. He later recounted what happened when he ventured down the corridor and met the garrison commander:

*Daring officers*

"'What are you doing here?' asked General Villa-Abraille.

33

*Opposite* Villagers raise their arms and wave white cloths in surrender as Rebel forces march into their village, September, 1936

B

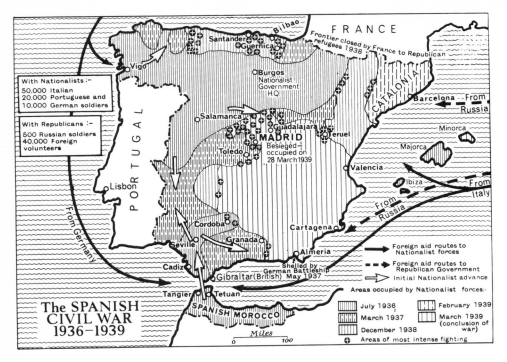

The SPANISH CIVIL WAR 1936–1939

With Nationalists:-
50,000 Italian
20,000 Portuguese and
10,000 German soldiers

With Republicans:-
500 Russian soldiers
40,000 Foreign volunteers

Foreign aid routes to Nationalist forces
Foreign aid routes to Republican Government
Initial Nationalist advance
Areas occupied by Nationalist forces:-

July 1936
March 1937
December 1938
February 1939
March 1939 (conclusion of war)
Areas of most intense fighting

MADRID
Besieged –
occupied on
28 March 1939

Shelled by German Battleship Gibraltar (British) May 1937

"'I have come to tell you the time has come to make a decision. Either you are with your comrades in arms, or you are with the government which is leading Spain to ruin.'

"'I shall always remain faithful to the government.'

"'Very well! I have the order of the military committee to blow out your brains, [but] . . . it will be enough to put you under arrest. Go back to your office.'

" . . . Then General López Vieta, his [Villa-Abraille's] chief of staff, said: 'Then I, too, must be put under arrest.'

"'Of course, if that's what you want,' I said.

"Then Colonel Hidalgo, who was also on the staff, said: 'I, too, should be arrested.'

"'I have no objection,' I said.

"So it was with the other officers. They were all placed in the room under arrest. I tore out the telephone wires, and was about to lock the door when I found there was no key. So I called a corporal and told him to shoot anyone who attempted to escape.

"'If anyone leaves this office, I shall have you shot,' I told him. And no one escaped . . . I had to rub my eyes to make sure I was not dreaming (41)." After taking the garrison, the General converted the entire city to the Rebel cause.

The Nationalist uprising could not be squashed by constitutional means because most of the forces which maintained law and order had deserted the government. Both the army and the civil guard, a police force which was virtually a separate army with a reputation for ruthlessness, had joined the Nationalists who claimed to represent law and order themselves. So the defence of the Republic depended upon the trade unions and left-wing political organizations. For several days the government refused to arm these groups as it feared a counter-revolution from the left. *The Republic undefended*

In Madrid the cry was "Arms, arms, arms." It was now that the Communist heroine, Dolores Ibarruri, usually known as *La Pasionaria,* made the first of her many violent speeches to rouse the *Madrileños* (people of Madrid). Always dressed in *La Pasionaria's exhortations*

*La Pasionaria*, the Spanish Communist leader, urging the *Madrileños* to resist the enemy

black, with a grave but fanatical face, she was regarded as a revolutionary saint by her followers. She urged armed resistance against the Nationalists with grim but stirring words which were to become Republican passwords in the months ahead. One of her most famous exhortations was: "It is better to die on your feet than to live on your knees! (42)"

Eventually, after a critical delay, the government gave arms to both the Anarchist and Socialist trade unions, the U.G.T. and C.N.T. Frequently, crowds of workers seized arms by force. In Madrid on 19th July, the Spanish journalist and author Arturo Barea reported: "Shouting and screaming, a tight cluster of people appeared on the other side of the Plaza de España. When the mass arrived at the street corner, I saw that it had in its midst a lorry with a 7·5 centimetre gun. Hundreds of people fell upon the lorry as though they wanted to devour it, and it disappeared beneath the human mass like a piece of rotting meat under a cluster of black flies. And then the gun was on the ground, lifted down on arms and shoulders (43)."

In several towns the Nationalist forces took over their own garrisons and although they could not control the surrounding areas, they were able to hold out for months against the Republican assaults. The most famous siege at this time was that of the Alcázar fortress in Toledo, forty miles from Madrid. Here a Nationalist force of 1,300 men with 600 women and children survived for over two months against a full scale Republican assault. The Republicans tried everything – a frontal attack, mining, spraying burning gasoline, and tossing hand grenades into the fortress – to force the Nationalists to surrender. During the siege, the son of the Nationalist commander, Colonel Moscardó, was captured. The Republican leader conducting the attack telephoned the Colonel and told him that unless the Nationalists surrendered, his son, Luis, would be shot. He then put the boy on the line:

*Siege of Alcázar*

" 'What is happening my boy?' asked the Colonel.

" 'Nothing,' answered the son. 'They say they will shoot me if the Alcázar does not surrender.'

" 'If it be true,' replied Colonel Moscardó, "commend your soul to God, shout "Viva España" and die like a hero. Goodbye

37

my son, a last kiss.'

" 'Goodbye father,' answered Luis, 'a very big kiss' (44)."

Luis Moscardó was shot on 23rd August. Four weeks later, a Nationalist column succeeded in raising the siege. The streets were soon running with the blood of Nationalist revenge.

*The "Terrors"* In the first two months of the Civil War, nearly a hundred thousand people were killed, most of them were massacred without trial off the field of battle. It was the time of the "Red" (Republican) and "White" (Nationalist) "Terrors." The Hungarian Arthur Koestler was a Communist journalist working for the Republican cause at this time. He defined the main reason for Nationalist atrocities: "The Spanish Rebels found themselves objectively in the position of an alien invading army. The masses sympathized either actively or passively with the opponents. There was only one method of forcing the masses in the districts which they took to become neutral; the method of terror . . . (45)"

A document found on a Rebel officer captured on 28th July, 1936, gives evidence of the Nationalists' policy of terror: "In order to safeguard the provinces occupied, it is essential to instill a certain salutary terror into the population (46)."

*Atrocities* A hotel employee, Jésus Corrales, gave an eyewitness account of the atrocities performed by the Nationalists: "In Seville, I saw with my own eyes the shooting of a group of about a hundred and fifty prisoners, amongst whom there were some women. In order to keep the population in a constant state of terror, General Queipo de Llano gave orders that the prisoners should not be shot, as at first, in the barracks, in the prison or the cemetery, but in the streets of working-class districts, and that the corpses should be left lying in the streets for from twelve to sixteen hours, after oil had been poured on them so as to avoid the possibility of epidemics (47)."

*Mass executions* Jésus Oyarzun, a farmer from Segovia, was another eyewitness who told his story to Arthur Koestler: "In Segovia mass executions take place at night in the cemetery. A searchlight and two machine guns are used. As a result of this summary procedure it often happens that men and women who are not yet dead but only wounded, are thrown into the mass grave. This

Cut off from their main force, a group of Republican troops are taken
captive by Nationalist soldiers

story has got round amongst the prisoners and their fear is that
they will be buried alive . . . I again and again saw individuals
usually women but sometimes men who were about to be shot –
throw themselves at the feet of the Falangists, clasp their arms
and feet and implore them – not to spare their lives, but to shoot
straight or, if possible, to shoot them out of hand (48)."

So the atrocities went on. The Red Terror was more spontaneous and less organized than the White. The Republicans'
motives were fear, revenge and bitterness. Although the Church
had not actually taken part in the uprisings, the most intensely
persecuted group were the clergy. At least 7,000 priests were
executed by the Republicans. Murder gangs, such as "The
Lynxes of the Republic," and "The Furies," were organized by
the Communists and Anarchists. They went to work with
ferocious cruelty. The parish priest of Torrijos, Don Liberio

*Torture of
priests*

39

Gonzáles Nonvela, was taken prisoner by one of these gangs. He told his captors:

" 'I want to suffer for Christ.'

" 'Oh, do you?' they answered, 'then you shall die as Christ died.'

"They stripped him and scourged him. Then they fastened a beam of wood onto his back, gave him vinegar to drink, and crowned him with thorns.

" 'Blaspheme and we will forgive you,' said a captor.

" 'It is I who forgive and bless you,' replied the priest.

"Eventually he was shot, facing his tormentors so that he could die blessing them (49)."

In the areas of Spain under Nationalist control, anyone who was a member of a left-wing party ran the risk of the firing squad. In Republican Spain, a man of wealth who did not wear working-man's clothes was likely to be shot. The Republican government curbed some of the violence of the Red Terror after the first few months of the Civil War. But the Nationalists continued to use terror as a necessary weapon. Both sides were so ferocious that many wounded men begged their friends to shoot them rather than leave them to be captured and shot by the enemy. Both sides in the Civil War seemed to be obsessed by death. The battle-cry of both the Anarchists and Falangists was "*Viva la muerte!*" ("Long live death!") Also, both flew a red and black flag – symbolizing blood and death.

*Nationalist Spain*    The army was predominant in Nationalist Spain. "Those who don't wear uniforms should wear skirts," ran the jibe. Military laws replaced normal justice, and the only political parties allowed were the Falange and Carlists. The Carlists wanted the Bourbon monarchy to be restored in Spain. Both parties were organized like military movements.

The atmosphere of a town held by the Nationalists was described by Arthur Koestler. At the beginning of the war, he entered the town of Vigo by posing as a right-wing journalist: "[The foreigner] notes, during his hour's walk, that the town is chock-full of troops; that all taxis and private cars are [marked] 'Requisitioned'; that the civilians slink timidly along by the walls, and that scarcely a single woman is to be seen on the

Franco addressing a crowd of supporters from the balcony of the Nationalist headquarters in Burgos. Beside him is General Cabenellas

streets. He sees two suspects, one with a bleeding nose, being
escorted into the Palace of Justice, and notices that the passers-
by anxiously look the other way, to avoid hearing or seeing
anything. He reads the notices posted up in the cafes: 'You are
requested not to talk politics,' and hears people talking in
hushed whispers – for there are spies everywhere (50)."

Karl Robson, a journalist who covered the Civil War for *The
Daily Telegraph*, described the Nationalists' rather amusing
attempts to prevent dangerous gossip in the town of Saragossa:
"We were not encouraged to ask questions. Printed warnings to
combatants not to talk shop had been laid beneath the glass
covers of the tables in the hotel lounge. One of them read, 'Do
not be indiscreet with the woman sitting beside you at the

moment; you may bring harm on your brothers at the front.'
Another ran, 'Do not drink too much, or you will raise the
hopes of those who wish to make you a victim of espionage'
(51)."

*Franco takes*    The Nationalists' formal centre of power was Burgos, the
*command* base of the ruling "junta" (administrative council) under
General Cabanellas. Real power, however, soon belonged to
General Franco who assumed sole command of the army in
September, 1936. As a Spanish historian wrote in 1931, the
army was well adapted to civil war: "It would be erroneous to
imagine the Spanish army as a huge military machine power-
fully organized to obtain the highest possible fighting efficiency
. . . The army is a bureaucratic machine which spends most of
the money paid to it in salaries for generals and officers, a lesser
amount in war material, and a still lesser sum in preparing for
war. The army, in fact, is more important as an instrument of
home politics than as a weapon of war (52)."

*The Rebel*    The army officers, who averaged one to every six soldiers,
*army* were enlisted men with a tradition of meddling in politics; most
of the troops were conscripts. In 1936 only five hundred
regular officers out of fifteen thousand fought for the Republic
and only one third of the forty thousand conscripts also remained loyal. Despite these large numbers the strength of the
Nationalist army lay in the Army of Africa. This army was
made up largely of Moors from Morocco. In 1936 the northern
part of Morocco belonged to Spain, although the Moors were
Spain's historic enemies and conquerors. The African army
was backed up by the notorious Civil Guard and the Spanish
Foreign Legion. The Foreign Legion consisted of Spaniards,
Portuguese, French and Germans and held an equally infamous
reputation for violence – it, too, used the motto "Long Live
Death."

   These troops were supported by the two militant political
parties, the Falange and the Carlists. The role of the Falange was
similar to that of the Gestapo in the Third Reich. One eyewitness commented: "They play a minor part in the actual
fighting, but they like to take over the duties of the police and
to supervise the carrying out of executions behind the line (53)."

The Carlists were organized into *Requetés* (an obscure term *The Carlists* coming from one of their marching songs). They were conspicuous for their red berets, their battle cry of *"Viva Cristo – Rey!"* ("Long live Christ the King!") and their fighting spirit. One *Requeté* was asked who should be told in case of his death:

"My father, José Mariá de Miquerarena, of the Montejurra militia, aged sixty-five.

"And if he should be killed too?

"My son, José Mariá de Miquerarena, of the Montejurra militia, aged fifteen (54)."

In Nationalist Spain, past history was frequently invoked as an appeal to patriotism. In August, 1936, the Monarchist flag was substituted for that of the Republic. "This is our flag, for which our fathers died a hundred times covered in glory," cried General Franco (55). Franco himself was described as *Caudillo*, a translation from the German *Fuehrer*, or leader. The slogan, "The Caesars are always victorious Generals," was scrawled on buildings.

As we have seen, the Spanish Church had business and *The Church* political interests, strong links with the past and an under- *supports the* standable wish for self-preservation. So the Church allied itself *Rebels* with the Nationalist cause. It dominated most of the communications in Nationalist Spain – the pulpit, radio and newspapers – and it used them to depict the Civil War as a crusade against infidels. Some religious ceremonies seemed to come from the Middle Ages: "About this time [the end of August, 1936] a procession with the Archbishop of Toledo at its head marched through the streets of Pamplona carrying an image of the Madonna del Pilar. When it was over, the image of the Madonna was set up in the middle of the principal square of the town, and the clergy were drawn up round it in military formation; after a short ceremony, sixty prisoners were shot 'to the honour and glory of the Virgin' and the accompaniment of a peal of bells (56)."

This letter, written by a Catholic priest in Valladolid to an English colleague, was printed in the *Nottingham Evening News* on 26th November, 1936. It reminds one of the Spanish Inquisition: "Communism . . . is to be burnt from the land. No false sentimentality. They are offered the Sacrament and shot. If they blaspheme the Sacrament, they are flogged before being shot. More than 3,000 have been shot here. Many to follow. Each case is scrupulously examined (57)."

Propaganda played a big part in the Spanish Civil War. Both sides used this weapon which Hitler was perfecting in Germany. Earlier, Hitler had written in *Mein Kampf* how a leader could tell outrageous lies to his people which would be believed: " . . . The very magnitude of a lie endows it with a certain element of credulity, for the broad masses of the people are at bottom more liable to be corrupted than to be consciously and deliberately bad; thus the very naïveté of their mentality makes them fall more easily victim to a great lie than a small one, since they themselves may sometimes lie on a small scale, but would be very much ashamed of lying on a grand scale (58)."

A statement broadcast on Radio Castile by General Mola shows that Hitler's doctrine had been understood. Whether it had the desired effect on the listeners is a different matter. "[The Republican President Azaña is] a monster who seems more the absurd invention of a darkly insane Frankenstein than the fruit of a love of a woman. Azaña must be caged up so that special brain specialists can study perhaps the most interesting case of mental degeneration in history (59)." This was of course more than a lie – it was ridiculous. But it was no more ridiculous than the official German Nazi line, put out in a brochure called "Moscow, the Hangman of Spain." The Nazis claimed that the Generals' uprising was a counter-revolution against the Communists. According to Germany the Communists had started the Civil War by plotting to over-throw the Second Republic.

At the same time, many Communist journalists like Arthur Koestler and Claud Cockburn put out propaganda for the other side. Cockburn, for instance, wrote a feature for the Comintern propaganda department in Paris. He said, tongue-in-cheek, that "it had emerged as one of the most factual, inspiring, and at the same time, sober pieces of war reporting I ever saw (60)." The trouble was Cockburn had not witnessed this particular incident; it was a completely fictitious event he had dreamed up for propaganda purposes.

Among the Nationalists, the war and the army were everything. They hardly considered the possibility of political and social change in their bid for power. What did the ordinary people who lived in Franco's Spain think of Nationalist ideals? After all, many of them "supported" Franco only because they happened to be living in areas that were taken by the Nationalists in July, 1936. There were resistance groups, like the one in Ernest Hemingway's novel *For Whom the Bell Tolls,* but most Spaniards in Nationalist Spain who did not willingly support Franco kept quiet. They valued their lives more than anything else.

Economically, Nationalist Spain was very healthy; its peseta was quoted by foreign banks at double the rate of the Republic's. Food was plentiful; although there were few manufactured goods available, the backing of most Spanish bankers and financiers meant much could be bought abroad. Life in Franco's Spain was not only more comfortable than life in the Republic, it was also safer. From early on in the war it appeared unlikely the the Republicans would attack much of Rebel Spain. Most people in Nationalist Spain were content to live in relative comfort.

*Living in comfort*

Like Nationalist Spain, the character of the Republic was based on its army. The "People's Army" was enthusiastic, idealistic and brave; disorganized, ill-disciplined and ill-equipped; handicapped by poor leaders and torn by political disputes. For the first few months of the war, it was not so much an army as a collection of "militias" – citizens' armies based on political parties or the trade unions. A journalist described how one militia was formed: "All sorts and conditions of men from half the towns and villages of Spain were in the long lines that shuffled slowly past the recruiting examiners, presenting first their union cards to be scrutinized in order to ensure that they were trade unionists in good standing, then stripping to be examined by the doctor for medical fitness." Then the men took an oath: "I, son of the people, citizen of the Spanish Republic, freely accept service as a militiaman. I promise the Spanish people and the Government of the Republic, elected as a result of the Peoples' Front election victory, that I will defend with

*Republican Spain*

my life democratic liberty and the cause of peace and progress, and bear honourably the title of militiaman (61)."

There were no official uniforms, though most soldiers wore corduroy knee breeches and a zipper jacket. Militias were recognized by their different flags – the hammer and sickle for the Communists; red and black for the Anarchists; and red, yellow, purple for the Republic, which was usually flown by militiamen from the Socialist U.G.T. In addition, the soldiers wore the initials of their trade union on their caps.

The Anarchists, particularly, were ill-disciplined. After all, to obey orders was against Anarchist thinking. The F.I.A., the political wing of the Anarchists, demanded the suppression of the salute, equal pay, and soldiers' councils. "We are not making war but revolution," they declared. This joke went round about the Anarchists' military code (62):

*An Anarchist army?*

"Para 1: There shall be no order at all.
"Para 2: No one shall be obliged to comply with the preceding paragraph."

The English left-wing writer, George Orwell, fought with one of these militias. He described his preliminary training in a Barcelona barracks: "Discipline did not exist; if a man disliked an order he would step out of the ranks and argue fiercely with the officer. The lieutenant . . . was a sincere and ardent Socialist . . . I remember his pained surprise when an ignorant recruit addressed him as 'Señor.' 'What! Señor? Who is that calling me Señor? Are we not all comrades?' I doubt whether it made his job any easier (63)."

The Communist troops at first formed part of the Fifth Regiment. Like the Anarchists, they were politically minded. Indeed, "Political Commissars" were appointed to remind the troops what they were fighting for. But the Communists were realists, and military aims and needs held first priority. Therefore they were well disciplined and better organized than the Anarchists. The Communists had able military leaders, such as ex-quarryman Enrique Lister, ex-woodcutter Juan Modesto and Valentin González known as *El Campesino* (The Peasant). Before long it became apparent that the Fifth Regiment was much more effective than the militias.

*Effective Communist troops*

*Opposite* George Orwell, one of the many left-wing sympathizers who fought in the International Brigades for the Republican cause

In February, 1937, the city of Malaga was lost to the Nationalists. This disaster spurred on the army reforms which the Republic had begun a few months earlier. The militias now came under the control of the General Staff in Madrid. Also, Political Commissars, nearly all Communists, were appointed to all militias. Finally, pay scales were introduced, so that officers were paid more than their men. In other words, ranks were beginning to be formed. The Anarchists were mortified. A militiaman in the Iron Column, which consisted mostly of ex-convicts, wrote: "One day the news that we had to be militarized descended on the crests of the Sierra like an icy wind . . . I felt my body become limp, for I could see clearly that the guerilla fearlessness that I had derived from the revolution would perish (64)."

But Durruti, the leading Anarchist, supported the change: "You mean officers should be appointed? Orders should be obeyed? An interesting idea. Difficult to introduce but let us see . . . " He later said: "I am against the discipline of barracks but also I am against the misunderstood liberty which helps cowards . . . In war, delegates have to be obeyed (65)."

By 1937, the Republican army numbered about 450,000 compared to the Nationalist army's 600,000. In addition, both armies had foreign detachments, which will be described in Chapter 3. The Republican army was still ill-equipped and torn by political disputes, but by now it was more efficient and less idealistic. Gradually, the revolutionary zeal of the Anarchists was over-powered by realistic Communist discipline.

This revolutionary zeal was strongest in the provinces of Catalonia and Aragon. The Anarchists and the genuinely revolutionary Communist organization, P.O.U.M. (*Partido Obrero de Unificación Marxista*), were most powerful here. George Orwell gave his impressions of the city of Barcelona, capital of Catalonia: "When one came straight from England the aspect of Barcelona was something startling and overwhelming. It was the first time I had ever been in a town where the working class was in the saddle. Practically every building of any size had been seized by the workers and was draped with red flags or with the red and black flag of the Anarchists; every

Crowds waiting for free meals at the Ritz Hotel in Barcelona, transformed into a public restaurant by the Republicans

wall was scrawled with the hammer and sickle and with the initials of the revolutionary parties; almost every church had been gutted and its images burnt. Every shop and café had an inscription saying it had been collectivized." Large estates, railways, factories and companies in Barcelona were taken over by the Socialist or Anarchist trade unions, the C.N.T. and U.G.T., and run by the union members on behalf of "the people." "In outward appearance," Orwell wrote, "it was a town in which the wealthy classes had practically ceased to exist. Practically everyone wore rough working class clothes, or blue overalls or some variant of the militia uniform. All this was queer and moving (66)."

Money was no longer circulated in many places controlled by the Anarchists. A French observer wrote: "Everyone can get what he needs. From whom? From the Committee of course . . . Payment is made not with money but with coupons. The principle whereby each inhabitant shall receive goods according to his needs is only imperfectly realized, for it is postulated that everyone has the same needs . . . Every family has received a

49

A Republican patrol in Barcelona sets out in a requisitioned bus to round up anyone not dressed in working men's clothes

card. This is purchased daily at the place of work; hence no one can avoid working . . . Everyone – the worker, the doctor, the businessman – receives coupons to the value of five pesetas for each working day. One part of the coupon bears the inscription 'bread' . . . the other part can only be exchanged for consumer goods (67)."

*An Anarchist's idea of justice* Some Anarchists actually entered the Republican government. The Anarchist Minister of Justice had a very permissive attitude towards criminals: "Justice must be burning hot, justice must be alive, justice cannot be restricted within the bounds of a profession . . . Let us admit here in Spain that the common criminal is not an enemy of Society. He is more likely to be a victim of Society. Who is there who says he dare not go out and steal if driven to it to feed his children and himself? Man, after all, does not proceed from God, but from the cave, from the beast. Justice, I firmly believe, is so subtle a thing that to interpret it one has only need of a heart (68)." In January, 1937, the Minister of Justice declared total amnesty for all crimes committed before the beginning of the War.

Civil marriages were instituted in Republican-held areas: "On Sunday morning, in the presence of numerous comrades, a simple and emotional scene occurred in the Transport Union. Two young people came together by free and spontaneous decision . . . Juan Freixas and Tomasa Costa . . . This union had one bond: love . . . The voice of our director, Liberto Callejas, sealed the Union when he told them, 'In the name of liberty, stay united!' (69)" Abortions were legalized during the first three months of pregnancy. These changes were very radical in Catholic Spain.

*Radical social changes*

In 1936, many villagers took the law of landownership into their own hands. In the province of Badajoz, "organized groups of workers, armed with ropes, spades, and other implements, mustered secretly and trooped out from 150 of the 163 villages in the Province; they proceeded – many of them on their donkeys, of course – to the neighbouring big estates and calmly marked out the strips which they proposed to occupy for cultivation . . . Then, after a lusty cry of 'Viva la Republica,' they marched back to their villages (70)."

*Villagers occupy land*

So, unlike Nationalist Spain, there was great social and economic change in areas controlled by the Republicans. This social and economic "revolution" was uncoordinated by the central government. It was strongest in the provinces of Catalonia, Aragon and parts of Andalusia. In these regions the Anarchists were most powerful and, with the exception of Andalusia, the War was farthest away. In the provinces of Madrid and Valencia the Socialists held more power than the Anarchists and were more cautious. Most people in these provinces supported the central government of the Republic which retained its authority.

What was President Azaña's Popular Front government doing all this time? Azaña himself, dispirited and unloved, moved to Barcelona where he became an aloof and absentée President. Largo Caballero, the Socialist labour leader, became Prime Minister in September, 1936. The Socialists were joined

*Coalition governments*

51

by the Communists in the "Government of Victory," the first time a Communist Party had taken office in the West. In May, 1937, Largo Caballero's coalition government fell. It was replaced by another coalition led by ex-doctor Juan Negrín, in which the Communists held more power.

In December, 1936, the Communists issued this manifesto (71):

"1. Complete power for the central government

"2. A regular organized army based on universal service

"3. 'Iron Discipline' in the rear guard

"4. Nationalization of the 'principal branches' of industry."

This doctrine attracted increasing support from the Spanish people who supported the Republican cause, because they saw the need for unity and discipline. In June, 1937, the Communist Party claimed a membership of 387,000. In addition, many members of the U.G.T. (now two million strong) and the old Republican Left backed the Communists.

The Communists became stronger because the coalition governments of the Republic were too weak. Although Caballero's government pushed through reforms in education, health and land-ownership, neither Caballero nor Negrín could control the regions. And the Anarchists, with their wild revolutionary zeal, were not suited to running a government. The Anarchists themselves admitted that, like their military methods, much of their social and economic programme was not really workable. One Anarchist wrote: "We wished the socialization of all wealth so that not a single individual would be left out of the banquet of life. We have now done something but we have not done it well. In place of the old owner we have substituted a half dozen new ones who do not always know how to organize as well as the old (72)."

*The Anarchists join the government*   In November, 1936, however, the first Anarchists had joined the Communists in Caballero's coalition government. For many Anarchists it was a bitter day, for in joining the government they were giving up their principles. One wrote later: "Our incorporation . . . meant either an act of historic audacity or a . . . correction of an entire history. For others, a governmental post could be the goal and satisfaction of measureless ambitions. For

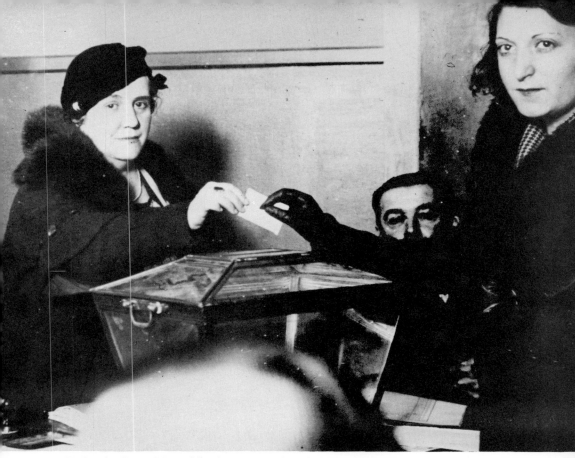

Under the Second Republic the women of Spain were able to vote for the first time. Here, a woman casts her ballot in the 1936 elections

me it was nothing less than a break with an entire life's work (73)."

By the end of 1936, the Republican government was less interested in revolutionary ideals and more concerned with the needs of a nation at war. Much property and business was nationalized, taxes were enforced and the authority of the government strengthened. In the *pueblos* (villages) municipal councils replaced political committees. On 6th November, 1936, Caballero moved the government away from Madrid, which was now under protracted siege, and installed it at Valencia. The Communists remained in Madrid, thereby increasing their popularity with the *Madrileños*.

53

In April, 1937, George Orwell went on leave after one hundred and fifteen days in the line. In Barcelona he found that the revolutionary spirit was on the decline. He wrote with resignation: "Of course such a state of affairs could not last. It was simply a temporary and local phase in an enormous game that is being played over the whole surface of the earth. But it lasted long enough to have its effect upon anyone who experienced it. However much one cursed at the time, one realized afterwards that one had been in contact with something strange and valuable. One had been in a community where hope was more normal than apathy or cynicism, where the word 'comrade' stood for comradeship and not, as in most countries, for humbug (74)."

# 3 Europe Intervenes

ON 19TH JULY, 1936, José Giral, who preceded Largo Caballero as Prime Minister of the Republic, sent a telegram to the Prime Minister of France, Léon Blum: "Are surprised by a dangerous military coup. Beg of you to help us immediately with arms and aeroplanes. Fraternally yours, Giral (75)." On the same day, Luis Bolin, a Nationalist agent who lived in London, flew to Rome on behalf of Generals Franco, Mola and Sanjurjo. He brought a request to Mussolini for twelve bombers, three fighters and some bombs. On the second day of the Civil War, therefore, both sides sought help from European governments.

*Both sides request aid*

Although Spaniards came to regret their actions, the fact was that they invited the European Powers into Spain. At the same time, the three Great Powers which took an active part in the War – Germany, Italy and the Soviet Union – did not require much persuasion. For they embodied the two ideologies which had brought Spain to the pitch of war – Fascism and Communism. More heroic and romantic were the forty thousand volunteers from all over Europe and America who joined the International Brigades on the side of the Republic. The Communist heroine *La Pasionaria* addressed the women of Barcelona and expressed in stirring words how these volunteers took up the Loyalist cause: "Mothers! Women! When the years pass by and the wounds of war are staunched; when the cloudy memory of the sorrowful, bloody days returns in a present of freedom, love and well-being; when the feelings of anger are dying away and when pride in a free country is felt equally by all Spaniards – then speak to your children. Tell them of the International

*The International Brigades*

Brigades. Tell them how, coming over seas and mountains, crossing frontiers bristling with bayonets, and watched for by ravening dogs thirsty to tear at their flesh, these men reached our country as Crusaders for freedom. They gave up everything, their loves, their country, home and fortune – fathers, mothers, wives, brothers, sisters and children, and they came and told us, 'We are here, your cause, Spain's cause, is ours. It is the cause of all advanced and progressive mankind' (76)."

*Europe decides on non-intervention*

But Europe did not at first heed *La Pasionaria's* cry. In August, 1936, twenty-seven nations, including Britain and France, formally agreed that they would not intervene in the Spanish Civil War. The model for their declaration was a note sent by the French Foreign Minister, Yvon Delbos, to the British Ambassador in Paris, Sir George Clerk. It contained three resolutions (77):

"1. The French government, in so far as it is concerned, prohibits direct or indirect exportation, re-exportation and transit, to a destination in Spain, the Spanish possessions or the Spanish zone of Morocco, of all arms, munitions and materials of war as well as all aircraft, assembled or dismantled, and all vessels of war;

"2. This prohibition applies to contracts in process of execution;

"3. The French government will keep the other governments participating in this entente informed of all measures taken by it to give effect to the present declarations."

Why did these nations formally agree not to send arms, and later soldiers, to Spain? Perhaps a more appropriate question, and one which the Republican government itself asked in the League of Nations, was why did these countries not intervene to support the loyal and legal government against the Rebel uprising? The answer was obvious, when one thinks of the increasing hostility between the Great Powers in the 1930s. As the Archbishop of Canterbury, Cosmo Gordon Lang, explained: "Mediation? Who can undertake the task? It would be a great thing if the leading European Powers would attempt it, but this might lead only to dissensions among themselves. Disquieting signs that the world seems to be going mad have come from

*Opposite* The British Prime Minister, Stanley Baldwin, supported the French policy of non-intervention in Spanish affairs

this horrible Civil War in Spain (78)."

Why was the Non-intervention Agreement signed with such speed by so many nations? One reason was that the Agreement was a moral commitment rather than an effective legal instrument. It was not binding on the nations who signed it. An international lawyer, Norman Padelford, noted: "It must be emphasized that the accord was not a formal international agreement or treaty in the sense that the participating states subscribed by signature and ratification to one written instrument. It was an accord only in a very loose form, a series of unilateral declarations of intention of the national policy which would be pursued (79)." *A moral commitment*

The loose form of the Agreement led one contemporary to give a rather cynical explanation: "The real truth was that all the interested Powers were only too anxious to play for time. In early September [1936] it was still impossible to decide which side in Spain would win, and Hitler and Mussolini were just as anxious as England not to make any too-decisive move. If the Fascist Powers too openly supported Franco, their prestige would suffer badly if he were defeated (80)." *Playing for time*

This is not to doubt the sincerity of France and Britain, the two leading Powers to sponsor non-intervention. Both the British Prime Ministers (Stanley Baldwin and later Neville Chamberlain) and the French Premier Léon Blum thought that European peace would be served best by preventing foreign military aid from reaching Spain. The majority of people in both countries were behind their leaders in thinking that involvement in Spain would increase the possibility of a European war. Even the arch-hawk Churchill at first agreed with this policy, which later turned out to be a policy of appeasement. When he was introduced to the Republican Ambassador in London, Pablo de Azcárate, "[Churchill] turned red with anger, muttered 'Blood, blood, blood,' and refused the Spaniard's outstretched hand (81)." *A policy of appeasement*

Non-intervention was a policy of appeasement because it was clear from the beginning that the committed nations intended to step in. The first signs of this hypocrisy were apparent when Germany, Italy and Portugal refused to take note of the preamble *Some nations step in*

59

*Opposite* Léon Blum, Prime Minister of France, feared that foreign intervention in Spain would bring about a European war

to the three French resolutions. The preamble declared (82):

"Deploring the tragic events of which Spain is the theatre; Resolved to abstain rigorously from all interference, direct or indirect, in the internal affairs of that country; animated by desire to avoid every complication which might prejudice maintenance of good relations between nations . . ."

The Portuguese government added a statement to its Declaration which was rather out of place in a note of neutrality: "The Portuguese government deplores the events which are taking place in Spain and it formally censures the barbarous treatment of people by the Communist and Anarchist troops in areas which they control (83)." German hypocrisy is shown by this letter, written on 29th August, 1936, by Dr. Hans Dieckhoff, acting State Secretary in the German Foreign Ministry: "I hardly believe that the plan [for setting up a Non-intervention Committee in London] could really entail any serious danger for us. The word 'control' does not appear in the French note . . . what was involved was primarily an exchange of information and co-ordination. We ourselves, after all, can play a part in seeing that this London arrangement does not develop into a permanent political agency which might make trouble for us; and in this we can secure Italian and British support, too (84)." The Italian representative on the London Non-intervention Committee, Count Dino Grandi, was in agreement with Berlin. He received secret instructions "to do his best to give the Committee's entire activity a purely platonic character (85)."

Behind this hypocritical facade, the committed nations supplied arms and men to Loyalists and Rebels. Britain and France reacted by adopting the policy of the "blind-eye," because it was the least trouble. One of the few ministers to disagree with the policy was the British Foreign Secretary Anthony Eden, who resigned on 20th February, 1938.

*The Non-intervention Committee*

Britain and France must bear the main blame for the failure of the non-intervention policy because in September, 1936, they took the initiative to set up the Non-intervention Committee to make sure the policy was carried out by all the Powers. The Committee was based in London. In January, 1938, the German representative on the Committee accurately described its work

60

*Opposite* Hitler and Mussolini, the leaders of European Fascism. It was their aid to General Franco that ensured his ultimate victory in the Spanish Civil War

as "unreal, since all participants see through the game of the other side, but only seldom express this openly. The non-intervention policy is so unstable, and is such an artificial creation, that everyone fears to cause its collapse by a clear 'no' and bear the responsibility. Therefore, unpleasant proposals are talked to death, instead of rejected (86)." By 1938 non-intervention was such a sham that Joachim von Ribbentrop, the German Ambassador in London, referred to the Committee as the "intervention committee."

The Spanish Republican government and the European Left watched the policy of non-intervention crumble. All they could see was Hitler and Mussolini arming the Rebels, and later bombing defenceless cities. Meanwhile, Britain and France denied aid to the legitimate government. Edgell Rickword, the editor of *Left Review*, wrote a poem called "To the Wife of any Non-intervention Statesman." It ended with this verse (87):

> *Would not a thinking wife condemn*
> *The sneaking hand that held the pen*
> *And with a flourish signed the deed*
> *Whence all these hearts and bodies bleed?*
> *Would not those fingers freeze the breast*
> *Where young life should feed and rest?*
> *Would not his breath reek of the tomb*
> *And would cold horror seal her womb?*
> *Could a true woman bear his brat?*
> *The millions wouldn't*
> *Thanks, my hat.*

*Hitler sends aid*     Herman Göring, Chief of the German Air Force (the *Luftwaffe*), stated at his trial in Nuremberg in 1946 how he had urged Hitler to support Franco: "When the Civil War broke out in Spain, Franco sent a call for help to Germany and asked for support, particularly in the air. Franco with his troops was stationed in Africa and . . . he could not get his troops across, as the fleet was in the hands of the Communists [the Republic] . . . I urged him [Hitler] to give support under all circumstances: firstly to prevent the further spread of Communism; secondly, to test my young *Luftwaffe* in this or that technical respect (88)." So the professed motive for the young Nazis who went to Spain

62

was stopping the spread of Communism. In the words of their marching songs: "We shall be marching onwards, if all else crashes about us. Our foes are the Reds, the Bolshevizers of the world (89)."

The transport of Germans troops, their arms and munitions *Secrecy fails* was carried out as secretly as possible. Bogus companies and tourist groups were set up to fool the Non-intervention Committee, the Republic and the suspicious European press. This secrecy was quite ineffective, particularly for journalists like Arthur Koestler who got into Nationalist Spain. Koestler wrote in 1937: "My private hobby was tracking down the German airmen; that is to say, the secret import of planes and pilots, which at that time [1936] was in full swing, but was not so

German troops march into Avila with soldiers of the Nationalist army

generally known as it is today. It was the time when European diplomacy was just celebrating its honeymoon with the Non-intervention Pact. Franco was denying having received them, while before my very eyes, fat, blonde German pilots, living proof of the contrary, were consuming vast quantities of Spanish fish, and, monocles clamped into their eyes, reading the *Voelkischer Beobachter* [the Nazi newspaper] (90)."

*The Condor Legion*

According to the historian Hugh Thomas, German aid to Franco amounted to about £43 million by 1939 exchange values. The total number of Germans who helped the Nationalists was about 16,000, of whom three hundred or so were killed. The Germans' manpower and arms commitment was to the Condor Legion, formed in 1936, which numbered six thousand men. Most regular formations of German forces fighting on Spanish soil, both infantry and airmen, belonged to this Legion. The commander of the Condor Legion was General Hugo Sperrle. He survived the Civil War, the Second World War (when he directed the German bomb attack on Coventry) and the Nuremberg War Trials. He died in 1953.

*Mussolini aids Franco*

Mussolini's support for Spain was more obvious than Hitler's but, considering all the Italian aid poured in, it was much less effective. Like Hitler, Mussolini was "not prepared to see the establishment of a Communist state" in Spain (91). And like Hitler he believed in a kind of empire-building which sounds very wrong to us today. Hitler had written in *Mein Kampf*: "A nation that aspires to be great is entitled to all the lands it may require; and this right becomes a duty when the nation sees in the extension of its territory a condition of its existence (92)."

Not that there is any evidence that Mussolini wished to conquer Spain in the way that he had conquered Abyssinia between 1935–1936. But he undoubtedly aimed to dominate the Mediterranean. This ambition would be furthered if Italy became co-victor in Spain and helped to set up a Fascist type of government. Moreover, militarism lay at the basis of Mussolini's beliefs. The following quotations from his speeches seem warmongering to us today, but in the 1930s they brought him huge support both in and outside Italy:

1932: "Fascism rejects pacifism as cowardice. War, and war only, brings to their maximum tension all human energies. Only war can give the seal of nobility to the peoples who have the courage to affront it (93)."

1936: "At the close of the year 14 [of the Fascist era] I raise a large olive branch. This olive branch rises from an immense forest: it is the forest of eight million bayonets well sharpened (94)."

And later: "When the war in Spain is over, I shall have to find something else: the Italian character has to be formed through fighting (95)."

So Mussolini wanted a war and Spain provided him with one. *Italian troops* While Hitler was discreet, Mussolini boasted openly about *in Spain* Italian military achievements in Spain. In March, 1937, when Italian troops were joining the Rebels in their attack on Madrid, Mussolini had this message circulated to all branches of the Italian army in Spain: "I will follow the fortunes of the battle with a tranquil soul because I am convinced that the enthusiasm and tenacity of our legionaries will sweep away the enemy's resistance. To defeat the international forces will be a success of the highest value, including political value. Let the legionaries know that I MYSELF am following their action from hour to hour and that it will be crowned with victory (96)."

The diary of an Italian officer captured in this campaign tells how the Italian troops felt about invading Spain. The officer describes his departure for Spain in January, 1937, in an Italian fleet guarded brazenly by Italian men-of-war: "Noiselessly the pirates of an ideal depart from their fatherland, on the most wonderful and most sacred adventure . . . The soldiers have been given amulets with the image of the Christ, the Holy Mother, and the Holy Ghost. The anxiety continues – after all, ours is a pirate ship. But our 'Papa' [Mussolini] is protecting us (97)."

The amulets were charms, probably similar to those given by the priests of Seville to Moorish troops to ward off bullets. Of course, they had no effect. Indeed, Italian troops, who were mostly conscripts or Fascist "blackshirts," were conspicuously battle-shy. Throughout the war, they were never able to live up to *Il Duce's* high expectations. The Madrid offensive, which

Mussolini was "following from hour to hour," was called off as a failure. The commanding officer, General Mancini, sent a very different message to his troops: "Cowards exist even in the best and bravest masses . . . but we must get rid of them.

"1. There have been cases of self-inflicted wounds;

"2. There have been cases of wounded and bandaged soldiers who, in fact, had nothing the matter with them;

"3. There have been cases where a genuinely wounded soldier was accompanied by others who were not . . . and took this chance to leave the firing line.

"ORDER: WHOEVER IS GUILTY OF ANY OF THE FOREGOING ACTS SHOULD BE IMMEDIATELY SHOT (98)."

According to Hugh Thomas, there was a maximum of 50,000 Italian troops in Spain in 1937; about 6,000 of them were killed. Italian arms sent to Spain included 760 aircraft, 950 tanks and $7\frac{1}{2}$ million rounds of artillery ammunition. The amount of monetary aid was about seven billion lire (£80 million; $200 million) by 1939 exchange values.

*Portugal supports the Nationalists*

The role of Portugal in the Civil War was simple. The government of Dr. Antonio Salazar was very similar in its aims and methods to the Nationalist government in Spain. Moreover, Portugal feared an invasion if the Left in Spain should win. So Salazar's government provided a refuge and a communications channel for the Nationalists. Gil Robles, the leader of the Catholic Party, and Franco's eldest brother, Nicolas, set up a headquarters for arms purchase in Lisbon. About 20,000 Portuguese volunteers fought for Franco in the Legion de Viriato and suffered about 8,000 casualties.

In addition, Hugh Thomas calculated that the Nationalist ranks were swelled by about 600 Irishmen, a dozen Britons, two Americans, a group of right-wing Frenchmen and a small number of Fascists from Eastern Europe.

*Stalin's policy*

The Republic did not receive nearly so much foreign aid as the Nationalists. France supplied a small amount of arms and munitions early in the war, and Mexico sent some money. But it was the Soviet Union who did most to help the Republic. The policy of its dictator, Josef Stalin, was more than complex; it was almost a contradiction. On the one hand he did not want a

66

*Opposite* Josef Stalin, the leader of Communist Russia, feared the establishment of a Fascist regime in Spain. But he also disliked the Trotskyist Communism of the Republicans

Nationalist victory. The Soviet Union, as the leader of world Communism, would obviously look with displeasure on a Fascist victory in Spain. Indeed, many Russians felt genuinely friendly towards the Republic. Moreover, Stalin had worked out a complicated political and military strategy – a Nationalist victory in Spain would threaten France; if French energies were directed towards protecting the country's southern frontier, Germany might be encouraged to attack Russia without fear of French retaliation. And Stalin was truly apprehensive of German intentions towards the Soviet Union.

On the other hand, Stalin did not want the Republic to win either. He realized that if the Republicans won, the Spanish government was likely to become Communist or Trotskyist and this, surprising though it may seem, thoroughly alarmed him. He knew that Britain and France would oppose a Communist Spain, and he did not want to arouse the enmity of these countries. He relied on them for common opposition against Germany. Stalin wanted to be the only leader of world Communism and a semi-independent Spanish Communist Party was not to his liking. Hence his policy was that neither side must win, but the war must go on.

*Secret Soviet aid*  Stalin's aid to the Republic had to be more secretive than German and Italian assistance to the Nationalists. He could not afford to disregard blatantly British and French wishes on the Non-Intervention Committee. Moreover, Stalin began to supply arms to the Republic in November, 1936, and by this time German and Italian troops were already fighting on the Rebel side. If Stalin's troops were recognized, there would really be an undeclared war in Spain between Germany, Italy and Russia. No wonder Stalin is reported to have warned his men: "Stay out of range of the artillery fire (99)."

So the vast bulk of Russian aid was food and raw materials. It was very helpful to the Republicans as the wheat and dairy areas of Spain had fallen to the Nationalists. Russia also supplied arms, and the nearest she came to admitting it was in this statement to the Non-Intervention Committee: "The Soviet government is therefore compelled to declare that if violations of the Agreement for Non-Intervention are not immediately stopped the Soviet government will consider itself free from the obligations arising out of that Agreement (100)."

In fact, nearly all the Soviet arms to Spain came through the Comintern in Moscow. The Comintern was the international organization for the spreading of Communist revolution throughout the world. Its arms chief was General Walter Krivitsky, who later defected to the West. His job was to use Comintern connections to buy arms wherever possible. He later wrote: "We made large purchases from the Skoda works in Czechoslovakia, from several firms in France, from others in Poland, and Holland. Such is the nature of the munitions trade that we even bought arms in Nazi Germany. I sent an agent representing a Dutch firm of ours to Hamburg where he had ascertained that quantities of somewhat obsolete rifles and machine guns were for sale. The director of the German firm was interested in nothing but the price, the bank references and legal papers of consignment (101)." *The Comintern supplies arms*

Krivitsky's "Republican Government's Arms Purchase Commission" attracted some very shady agents who organized payment for the arms, and their collection and delivery. One agent, named Ventoura, was "of Jewish origin. Born Constantinople. Found guilty of a swindle in Austria. False passport. Lives with a woman in Greece. Domicile in Paris in a hotel in Avenue Friedland (102)."

The "Republican Government's Arms Purchase Commission" was so called because the Republic paid for its arms and most other supplies. It had to pay for a very surprising reason: in the autumn of 1936, Largo Caballero, the Prime Minister, feared a rapid Rebel advance on Madrid. So he gave the order to Juan Negrín, then the Minister of Finance, to move the Bank of Spain gold reserves from Madrid "to the place which, in his opinion, offers the best security (103)." Negrín decided that the most secure place was the Soviet Union. Alexander Orlov was the chief Russian Security Officer in Spain who also defected to the West. He later wrote: " . . . As the military situation deteriorated, Negrín, in desperation, stretched his authority. He sounded out our Soviet trade attaché about storing the gold in Russia. The envoy cabled Moscow, and Stalin *Spanish gold shipped to Russia* leaped at the opportunity (104)." Apparently Stalin said, "They will never see their gold again, just as they do not see their own ears (105)." Orlov's first quotation comes from his own article in the *Reader's Digest* of November, 1966. It is called, "How Stalin Relieved Spain of $600,000,000." Certainly this money was never returned by the Soviet government.

Much of the money was spent on war materials for the Loyalist cause. Whatever the cost of these arms and munitions, few at the time doubted that they were indispensable to the Republic. Ninety per cent of the Loyalist Air Force, most of the tanks, a further 10,000 vehicles and 15,000 tons of fuel came from foreign Communists between 1936–38.

*Stalin's agents*    Stalin's political aim in supplying arms was "to include Spain in the sphere of the Kremlin's influence (106)." As stated above, he did not want an independent Communist or Trotskyist government there. To carry out his policy, he sent two faithful Communists to Spain. One was Palmiro Togliatti, the devious leader of the banned Italian Communist Party, who ran the Comintern in Spain. The other was Vladimir Ovseyenko Antonov, the Russian hero who had led the Red Guards in the storming of the Winter Palace in Moscow in 1917, and was now made the Soviet Consul General in Madrid. Stalin gave them an unenviable task. They were to ensure that the Communists only defended the Republican government and did not demand further socialization of industry or expropriation of landlords.

*The*    The real Communist revolutionaries, the Trotskyist party or
*Trotskyites*    P.O.U.M., were outraged. They called Stalin a "liquidator
*purged*    and traitor of the Spanish Revolution, abettor of Hitler and Mussolini (107)." In effect the Kremlin waged a civil war within the Spanish Civil War. The P.O.U.M. was purged in the province of Catalonia and its formidable leader, Andrés Nin, was hideously tortured; "At the end of a few days, his face was no more than a formless mass (108)."

*"The god that*    Many Spanish leaders were disgusted with the whole affair.
*failed"*    Largo Caballero fell from power because he refused to join in the suppression of the P.O.U.M. José Diáz, the Secretary-General of the Spanish Communist Party, spoke of "this
70    spiritual death (109)" of the Party. In the end, Stalin's policy

did not save the respectability of the Republic, and still antagonized Britain and France. For many Communists, like Arthur Koestler, the Spanish Civil War caused their final disillusionment with Russia – their "god had failed," when put to the test. Antonov himself was recalled to Russia and disappeared in Stalin's purges.

But the main work of the Comintern in the Civil War was to raise the International Brigades. These were volunteer forces who fought for the Republic and greatly strengthened the Loyalist cause. They were recruited and organized by European Communist parties. About sixty per cent of the 40,000 men who became volunteers were Communists before the Civil War began. Stalin and the Comintern supported the Brigades because they were good propaganda, a source of recruits and a possible nucleus of an international Red Army. *Volunteers from many nations*

Whether Communist or not, the volunteers went to Spain for the sake of an ideal. One enthusiastic volunteer wrote: "What is happening here is really the greatest thing since 1917 [the Russian Revolution]. Victory means the end of Fascism everywhere sooner or later, and most likely sooner (110)." *Fighting for an ideal*

In his book *English Captain* Tom Wintringham, an English Communist who served first with a British medical unit, said of his fellow volunteers: "They had come to Spain because they believed that Fascist aggression must be resisted, when need be, with lead and steel as well as with argument and propaganda (111)."

The Englishman Herbert Read, who also served in a medical unit, dedicated this poem to the Spanish Anarchists (112):

> *The golden lemon is not made*
> *but grows on a green tree:*
> *A strong man and his crystal eyes*
> *is a man born free.*
>
> *The oxen pass under the yoke*
> *and the blind are led at will;*
> *But a man born free has a path of his own*
> *and a house on the hill*
>
> *And men are men who till the land*

71

*and women are women who weave:*
*Fifty men own the lemon grove*
*and no man is a slave.*

These sentiments show why the Spanish Civil War was "the last great cause" for so many people. Over eighty per cent of volunteers who joined the Brigades were working class and they identified with the ordinary Spanish men and women in their struggle for freedom. The English poet, John Cornford, wrote this description of a Spanish village: "One of the things I remember most vividly is how, when we marched into Tierz, three miles from Huesca, in spite of the fact that they had been deluged with stories of rape and atrocity by the retreating Fascists, the villagers came out into the Market Square to welcome us, and took us off to their houses, where they had already prepared meals, and beds in the straw. In one village we passed through, the People's Committee had taken a voluntary decision to continue paying their normal rents – to the militia (113)."

*Troop trains*    The main recruiting office of the Brigade was in the rue de Lafayette in Paris. One of the men working there was Josip Broz, now President Tito of Yugoslavia. The usual route into Spain was by train from the Gare d'Austerlitz via the cities of Perpignan and Barcelona to the barracks at Albacete. George Orwell described the journey: "[It was] practically a troop train, and the countryside knew it. In the morning, as we crawled along southern France, every peasant working in the fields turned round, stood solemnly upright, and gave the anti-Fascist salute. They were like a guard of honour, greeting the train mile after mile (114)."

*The battalions*    On arrival at Albacete, volunteers were identified and registered. Those with special training, such as cooks, typists and machine-gunners, were singled out. Then the volunteers were divided into companies, according to language. The companies were formed into battalions, which were named after past Communist heroes. For example, there was the XI Brigade (in fact this was the 1st Brigade but numbering started at eleven, possibly to disguise how few there were) consisting mostly of Germans, French, Poles, Hungarians and Yugoslavs. It was

72

English members of the International Brigades at a machine gun post on
the Aragon front, June, 1938

divided into the Edgar André Battalion, the Commune de Paris
Battalion and the Dabrowsky Battalion. There were seven
Brigades in all. The British contingent numbered about 2,000 of
whom 500 were killed and 1,200 wounded. The British initially
made up "No. 1 Company" attached to the French Marseillaise
Battalion of the XIV Brigade. Volunteers came from fifty-three
nations; France and Germany supplied the most. About one-
third lost their lives and many more were later to suffer because
of their political and military allegiance to the Spanish Republic.

Herbert Matthews, who reported the war for the *New York
Times*, described two volunteers: "Hans is thirty-eight or
thirty-nine, married, tall, dark. Before the [First] World War he
was a cadet in a military school, for he comes of a good family.
During the war he was an officer in the German Army, and he

*Two
volunteers*

73

Cooks at a field kitchen prepare food for members of the International Brigades. Shortage of rations was a crucial problem for the Republicans

fought well. But what he saw then made him hate nationalism, and he became a journalist for radical newspapers. In the struggle against Hitler he was on the losing side and had to leave Germany. During the Asturian revolt here in 1934, Hans came to Spain to help the miners . . . So when the Civil War started, Hans had no hesitation. Leaving his wife and job in France, he came here, as he says 'to defend liberty.'

"And then there was Oliver Law, a Texas Negro, and commander of the Lincoln Battalion. A Negro commander of a hundred and fifty white men who were proud to serve under him – does that not convey something of the spirit of the Internationals? Law was in some sense the typical Negro radical. Sensitive and rebellious against the fate of his people in the South, he naturally drifted into the [Communist] movement. A good businessman to boot, he owned a restaurant and other property, which he gave up to come to Spain. And here he died, leading his men in an attack. 'We are here to show that Negroes know how to fight Fascists,' he said one day (115)."

Oliver Law was one of 1,000 American volunteers who died in Spain. Of the 2,800 Americans who joined the International Brigades, many were Negro or Jewish: "I know what Hitler is doing to my people," a Jewish-American volunteer told the *Life* magazine correspondent. Most of the Americans fought in the Abraham Lincoln Battalion, which was part of the XV Brigade. It was the only Battalion in which the majority of soldiers were students.

The Abraham Lincoln Battalion came to a sad end. Six hundred of its veterans fought in the Second World War, and the survivors held a reunion in 1946. But anti-Communist feeling ran so high in America that shortly afterwards the Battalion was declared subversive and disbanded.

The International Brigades were firmly managed by the Comintern and behind that organization, by Russia. Political Commissars were attached to most Companies and overall command was vested in a *Troika* of Communists, one Frenchman and two Italians. The military commander was the Frenchman, André Marty. This was a dreadful mistake as Marty was an inadequate soldier, arrogant, cruel and suffering from a paranoic suspicion of Fascist and Trotskyist spies. In Ernest Hemingway's *For Whom the Bell Tolls*, he is given the fictional name of "Comrade Massart": ". . . His grey face had a look of decay. His face looked as though it were modeled from the waste material you find under the claws of a very old lion . . .

*André Marty*

" 'He may be a glory and all,' the Corporal said . . . 'but he is as crazy as a bedbug. He has a mania for shooting people.'

" 'Truly shooting them?'

" '*Como lo oyes* ['as you hear it'],' the Corporal said. 'That old one kills more than the bubonic plague. But he doesn't kill Fascists as we do. He kills rare things. Trotskyists. Any type of rare beasts' (116)."

Any suggestion of political disagreement, military opposition, ill-discipline or cowardice was enough for Marty to order execution. His unchecked tyranny was the cause of disillusionment and the lowering of morale throughout the Brigades. He survived the war and was only excluded from the Communist Party just before his death in 1955.

*Troubles in the Brigades*

There were other troubles too: bad food, lack of uniforms and equipment, national and political rivalry and the loss of enthusiasm as the war progressed. These troubles caused many desertions and a falling off in recruitment. The English poet, Stephen Spender, tried to escape and was almost shot. He expressed the awareness of the waste of the war in this verse: (117):

> *O too lightly he threw down his cap*
> *One day when the breeze threw petals from the trees.*
> *Consider. One bullet in ten thousand kills a man.*
> *Ask. Was so much expenditure justified*
> *On the death of one so young, and so silly*
> *Lying under the olive trees, O world, O death?*

*Tightening up discipline*

In the summer of 1937, at the Battle of Brunete, some of the Brigades mutinied. Soon after, Marty was summoned to Russia to explain his conduct. Some of the leading officers were purged and the Communist grip was tightened. Moreover, the Brigades were formally incorporated into the Republican army and far more attention was paid to discipline and dress. *Our Fight*, a weekly newspaper in English published by the XV Brigade, spent a lot of space justifying the salute (118):

"1. A salute [the anti-Fascist clenched fist] is the military way of saying 'hello'.

"2. A salute is the quickest way for a soldier to say to an officer 'What are your orders?'

"3. A salute is a proof that our Brigade is on its way from being a collection of well-meaning amateurs to a steel precision instrument for eliminating Fascists."

Despite their internal problems, the International Brigades played a crucial role in the defence of the Republic. Their commitment to the cause, their bravery and organization, and their very presence in such large numbers strengthened the will power and military defenses of Republican Spain. Their withdrawal in November, 1938, was one reason why these defenses fell.

# 4 The Siege of Madrid

AFTER THE ARRIVAL of German and Italian aid in the autumn of 1936, Generals Mola and Franco felt strong enough to lay plans to capture Madrid. There was only thirty kilometres or so of weakly defended territory separating the Rebel and Loyalist lines. The new German Condor Legion was eager to bomb the defenseless capital. The Nationalists were supremely confident that not only would Madrid fall by the end of the year, but that the Republican government would fall with it. Radio Lisbon even broadcast an imaginary description of General Franco entering Madrid on his white horse. Nationalist confidence was bolstered by the knowledge that many people in the city sympathized with their cause. When General Mola was asked which of his four columns or armies, would take Madrid, he replied that the responsibility would lie with his "Fifth Column" of secret supporters in the capital (119). This is how the term "Fifth Column" passed into the dictionary. It now means any group of secret sympathizers who work for the enemy behind the lines.

The Nationalists launched heavy bomb attacks from 29th October onwards to weaken the city for their offensive. Certainly, morale in Madrid was low. The government had fled, leaving General José Miaja in charge. But he was just a figurehead – the Communists really directed the administration. The Spanish writer Arturo Barea described the atmosphere: "In those days of November, 1936, the people of Madrid, all of them together, and every single individual by himself, lived in constant danger of death. The enemy stood at the gates of the city and could

*Low morale in Madrid*

77

Citizens waiting for their ration of water during the Nationalists' siege of Madrid

break in at any moment. Shells fell in the streets. Bombers flew over the roofs and dropped their deadly loads, unpunished . . . No one knew for certain who was a loyal friend and who a dangerous hidden enemy. No one was safe from denunciation and error, from the shot of an over-excited miliciano [militiaman] or of a masked assassin dashing past in a car and spraying the pavement with machine-gun bullets. What food there was might disappear overnight. The air of the town was laden with tension, unrest, distrust, physical fear, and challenge, as it was laden with the unreasoning, embittered will to fight on. We walked side by side, arm in arm, with death (120)."

Madrid was the first great city to be the victim of an indiscriminate bombing campaign. Over a thousand inhabitants were killed. As the Germans realized, it was a foretaste of what was to happen on a larger and wider scale during World War Two a few years later. But at least London and the Ruhr were capable of putting up some ground-to-air defence against the

*Constant bombing*

*Opposite* A camp of the German Condor Legion in Spain. Notice the signs in German

Nationalist troops resting on the march to Madrid, November, 1936.
The battle for Spain's capital was a long and bitter struggle

bombs. Mikhail Koltzov, a Russian soldier who was Hemingway's model for "Kharkov" in *For Whom the Bell Tolls*, left these impressions of the bombing of Madrid: "Every three or four hours the bombardment is renewed. After each bombing there are more and more blazing ruins, more and more heaps of bloody flesh. The prayers, screams and lamentations of the people rise from the street. Those sharp-sighted, quietly murderous men manning their dark grey, steely planes circle the city, and the rumble of death can be heard above the defenseless roofs . . . What seemed to be an ominous shape of the future, recorded only in books, has become fact (121)."

The Battle of Madrid opened on 8th November, 1936. It was

*The battle begins*

an extraordinary conflict between two armies which both incorporated troops from many foreign countries. The Nationalist army of 20,000 consisted mainly of Moroccans and Legionaries, supported by Germans and Italians. Against them was an ill-armed urban mass backed up by Russian munitions. The International Brigades arrived at a crucial moment – the day the siege became an offensive – to boost the morale of the Republicans and their firepower. The XI and XII Brigades were distributed among the Spanish units to provide expertise and backbone. But it was the bravery of the *Madrileños,* spurred on by the invective of the heroine *La Pasionaria* and others like her, which eventually repulsed the Rebels. "Over the crackle of fire, there could be heard the monotonous refrain, repeated syllabically, like a beat on a distant drum, '*No pas-ar-an! No pas-ar-an! No pas-ar-an!*' They shall not pass! (122)" The air attacks stiffened this determination to resist, an unexpected reaction which was to be repeated in World War Two.

The main battleground was the University City at the north-east corner of Madrid, the one area where the Nationalists were able to maintain a foothold. Here they had broken through after an uncharacteristic retreat by Durruti's Anarchists, who had recently arrived from Catalonia. The battle scene was eerie. After the pounding of the aerial bombardment, Rebels and Loyalists grappled in hand-to-hand fighting. They struggled to gain control of floors and even rooms in libraries, laboratories and hostels of the University. "In the clinical hospital, the Thaelmann Battalion [of the XI International Brigade] placed bombs in lifts, to be sent up to explode in the faces of the Moroccans on the next floor. And, in that building, the Moroccans suffered losses by eating inoculated animals kept for experimental purposes (123)." As the battle continued, the Loyalist troops were forced from room to room and floor to floor, until they held only the Hall of Philosophy and Letters. Here the Englishman John Sommerfield "learned a new kind of fighting, the shooting amongst buildings, the machine-gun duels between men behind barricaded windows two hundred yards apart . . . We built barricades with sand-bags, with furniture, with books: we found sofas to sleep on: in the night we dug

*Fighting floor by floor*

81

communication trenches between buildings, and made tunnels under the roads . . . we lay down on velvet cushions beside our guns: we sniped from arm-chairs: and at night there were bombing parties (124)." The struggle for the University City ended on 23rd November in a stalemate. Both sides dug trenches and the battlefield took on the air of World War One.

The Battle of Madrid started again in mid-December. The Nationalists' aim was now to consolidate their foothold by cutting off the capital from the north. They planned to capture the Madrid–Corunna road and occupy the Sierra Mountains.

The Nationalist troops ran into their first opposition at the *pueblo* of Boadilla, thirty kilometres from the capital. They took the village after the Republican opposition collapsed under a massive shelling by the artillery, and then bombardment by German planes. Esmond Romilly, a nephew of Winston Churchill, was one of eighteen Englishmen who took part in the Battle of Madrid. Only two of them survived, and Romilly wrote later in his book, *Boadilla:* "The time you are a real pacifist is the time you know real sickening fear. That was as near any of us got to being pacifists (125)." *Battle of Boadilla*

During the next thirty days, there were many hard-fought but wasteful attacks and counter-attacks. Between 5th and 15th January alone there were 15,000 casualties on both sides. At one stage in the fighting, the Republican ammunition supply was so low that General Miaja had to send blanks up to the line. He hoped that if the soldiers heard their rifles firing they would go on defending themselves. By 15th January, exhaustion and losses on both sides had led to another stalemate. By this time, the Nationalists had pushed their front ten kilometres along the Madrid–Corunna road. They were now just short of the city of Majadahonda. The Nationalist arrowhead advance was now a wedge, but Madrid was still not isolated from its northern approaches.

During these weeks of fighting two Englishmen were killed whose poetry and prose have now reached the stature of the best war literature. They were the poet John Cornford and the prose-writer Ralph Fox. Like Romilly and probably all untried volunteers, Cornford had worried earlier how he would react *War poetry*

*Opposite* Men of Spain's Foreign Legion drawn up to attack a small village on the outskirts of Madrid under fire (126):

> *Then let my private battle with my nerves,*
> *The fear of pain whose pain survives,*
> *The love that tears me by the roots,*
> *The loneliness that claws my guts,*
> *Fuse in the welded front our fight preserves.*

By the first dreadful winter of the Civil War, there was a 2,000 kilometre boundary between Rebels and Loyalists. Small battles, sorties and sniping took place on the battle-fronts which made up the boundary. George Orwell described the front which he defended with his unit of P.O.U.M. militia: "[It was] a system of narrow trenches hewn out of the rock with extremely primitive loopholes made out of piles of limestone. Twelve sentries were at various points in the trench, in front of which was the barbed wire, and then the hillside slid down to a seemingly bottomless ravine; opposite lay naked hills (127)."

*Soldiers' lives* For the soldiers, there were more important considerations than the enemy. "In trench warfare," Orwell reported, "five things are important: firewood, food, tobacco, candles and the enemy. In winter on the Zaragoza front they were important in that order, with the enemy a bad last (128)." Orwell bore out the saying that "three-quarters of a soldier's life is spent in aimlessly waiting about." He wrote: "Up here, in the hills round Zaragoza, it was simply the mingled boredom and discomfort of stationary warfare . . . Sentry-go, patrols, digging; digging, patrols, sentry-go. On every hill-top, Fascist or Loyalist, a knot of ragged, dirty men shivering round their flag and trying to keep warm. And all day and night the meaningless bullets wandering across the empty valleys and only by some rare improbable chance getting home on a human body (129)."

*Malaga falls* On 8th February, 1937, General Queipo de Llano and his Nationalist troops captured Malaga, a major city in the south with 100,000 inhabitants. Arthur Koestler had realized how fragile Malaga's defenses were when he had inspected its one strategic road to the front, the road to Gibraltar. He had seen no trenches, no fortifications and few soldiers: "Where are your troops?" he had asked one of the sentries.

"Somewhere in the barracks. If the Rebels were to attack, we

Republican soldiers bring their artillery into position for an attack on
a Nationalist stronghold

should see them and have plenty of time to warn our men. Why
should they sit out in the rain?" The soldier admitted that they
had no tanks but added, "We shall strangle them with our
naked hands (130)."

When the attack came on 3rd February, the Republican
troops offered no resistance. With the political leaders, they
were the first to flee up the coast. The people of Malaga were
left defenseless against the rampaging Nationalist and Italian
troops. Arthur Koestler, who was in the city, was captured and
imprisoned for several months. He expected all the time to be
executed. Many people managed to escape from the town by the
road to Almeria. Nationalist tanks and aircraft pursued these
refugees. The soldiers let the women go free because more
hungry mouths would burden the dwindling Republican food
supplies. But they shot the men in sight of their families. The

Englishman T. C. Worsley drove a mobile blood-transfusion unit on this front. His description of the flight from Malaga expresses harrowingly the human tragedy of war: "The lorry was packed full, tight to suffocating, and still the people below pressed round it entreating and beseeching.

" 'Not for me, *companero*, it's not for me I'm asking. But take the child, save my child.' 'Holy Mary, save the little one.' 'Mother of God, don't leave my child.'

"They put their arms round me; they fell to the ground and clutched my knees, holding up their babies, and imploring my compassion.

"From out of a house came a man carrying in his arms a little boy, unconscious with a high fever. 'He's dying,' the man said, 'you must take him, you must. You can't leave him here to die.' Tears were running down his brown, wrinkled face; the mother followed, weeping, too; with a baby sucking at her breast. She looked at me dumbly, imploring . . . (131)"

*Battle of Jarama Valley*

The easy victory at Malaga encouraged the Nationalists to launch two new major offensives against Madrid. The first was concentrated south-east of the city in the valley of the Jarama River. The aim of the offensive was to sever the Madrid–Valencia road. The attack covered an eighteen kilometre front which ran north-south and started within twelve kilometres of the capital.

The battle began on 12th February and ended two weeks later in a stalemate similar to that at the Corunna road. Both sides were exhausted yet still strong enough to repulse any attack by the other. The territorial result was similar too. The Nationalists had managed to push their front across the Jarama River into a bulge about fifteen kilometres deep. But the Republicans had prevented them from gaining their real objective, the Valencia road. So both sides claimed a limited victory. The battle was marked by one new and heartening feature for the Republicans – their Russian fighters dominated the air for the first time.

*"Suicide Hill"*

Losses were heavy – over 20,000 on both sides. The British Battalion under Captain Tom Wintringham fought together for the first time. Only 225 out of the 600 strong Battalion survived, and only 80 or so were not wounded. One of their tasks was to defend "Suicide Hill" against artillery and machine-gun fire from the heights above them. John Lepper, one of the surviving British volunteers, wrote later (132):

> *Death stalked the olive trees*
> *Picking his men*
> *His leaden figure beckoned*
> *Again and again.*

Scotsman Alex MacDade recorded the feelings of the survivors of "Jarama Valley" (133).

> *There's a valley in Spain called Jarama,*
> *That's a place that we all know so well,*
> *For 'tis there that we wasted our manhood*
> *And most of our old age as well.*

Despite the cynicism of "Jarama Valley," the poetry that came out of the Civil War shows the emotional depth and intellectual powers of many of the volunteers who fought. The War made poets of some men who had never written before and would never do so again. This expressive poem was found scribbled in the notebook of one unidentified corpse (134):

> *Eyes of men running, falling, screaming*
> *Eyes of men shouting, sweating, bleeding*
> *The eyes of the fearful, those of the sad*
> *The eyes of exhaustion, and those of the mad.*
> *Eyes of men thinking, hoping, waiting,*
> *Eyes of men loving, cursing, hating,*
> *The eyes of the wounded sodden in red,*
> *The eyes of the dying and those of the dead.*

The last major Nationalist offensive against Madrid began on 8th March, 1937. Rebel troops launched an attack from the north-east. Their aim was to capture the provincial capital of Guadalajara, eighty kilometres from the capital, and then advance further south-west to meet up with the Jarama offensive. Hence Madrid would be encircled. The Nationalist army of 50,000 was a mixed force consisting of Moroccans, Carlists, Legionaires and 30,000 Italian conscripts fresh from the easy conquest of Malaga. Against this force General Miaja threw

87

The battles around Madrid, November, 1936, to March, 1937

seasoned troops led by the Communist commanders *El Campesino* and Hans.

*Battle of*     The two armies confronted each other at the town of Brihuega.
*Brihuega*   There were Italian soldiers fighting on both sides. Four divisions fought with the Nationalists – the Black Shirts, Black Flames, Black Arrows and Littorio Division; the Garibaldi Battalion of refugees from Mussolini's Italy fought for the Republic. Propaganda played an important part in the battle, as each side tried to win over more Italian soldiers. Standing in the battle line, the German Gustav Regler, a Political Commissar, reported: "It was the loudspeakers to speak first . . . 'Italian brothers, the Spanish people are fighting for their freedom. Desert the ranks of their enemies! Come over to us! We will welcome you as comrades-in-arms, we, the men of the Garibaldi Battalion.'" As the loudspeakers were blaring, the battle raged on: "A bullet burst against the wall where I was standing with

the French, waiting to see what effect this would have.

"'Not a bad full-stop!' said Boursier, their youthful commander (135)."

After ten days the Italian Fascists retreated. The retreat developed into a humiliating rout – 2,000 Italians were killed and 4,000 wounded. The Loyalists were of course overjoyed by the defeat of the Italians, and many Rebels were far from sorry. Many of them resented Mussolini and his plans to dominate Spain. Herbert Matthews, a journalist who covered the war for the *New York Times*, noted the Rebels' attitude: "What they [the Loyalists] had defeated was an Italian force, not a Spanish insurgent army. The loss and shame was Italy's, not Franco's, and I fully believe the stories told of rejoicings in Salamanca [the Falangist and diplomatic centre] . . . at the defeat of the hated foreigners." Matthews then explained how the Loyalists viewed their triumph: "The victory was not national, but international: the anti-Fascists had defeated the Fascists – that was the chief significance of Brihuega (136)." Mussolini was enraged. Signor Grandi, the Italian Ambassador in London, declared that "not a single Italian volunteer would leave Spanish soil before the end of the Civil War (137)." *The Italians routed*

The clear proof that Italian units were fighting for the Nationalists and the rout of these troops was of great propaganda benefit to the Republic. Otherwise, the result was another stalemate. The Nationalists failed to encircle Madrid, but they did advance their territory a further twenty kilometres. Guadalajara was the last of the series of Nationalist offensives against Madrid. Later in the war, the Republic re-opened the front in an attempt to lift the siege.

By the end of March, 1937, the Rebels had added much of Andalusia to the parts of Spain they had over-run the previous July. But after their failure to capture Madrid, they realized that the war would not be won quickly. They therefore decided to boost morale by mopping up the isolated Republican enclave in the North. And so began the "Basque Tragedy." The English poet C. Day Lewis expressed his feelings in this verse (138): *The "Basque Tragedy"*

*Freedom is more than a word, more than the base coinage*

*Of statesmen, the tyrant's dishonoured cheque, or the dreamer's mad*
*Inflated currency. She is mortal, we know, and made*
*In the image of simple men who have no taste for carnage*
*But sooner kill and are killed than see that image betrayed.*

But the Basques had little chance. A journalist wrote: "The northern enclave was badly supplied with arms, and had no air force, and must fall ultimately from an assault by a properly equipped army (139)." Moreover, the Republic was loath to send reinforcements, even if they could get through the sea blockade set up by the Rebel navy. The Republicans realized that the fate of the Basque provinces would not settle the war, and the Communists did not like the essentially Catholic character of the "Basque experiment." Finally, many people thought that if the Basques insisted on governing themselves, they must also be self-sufficient.

The Basque fight, then, was heroic but helpless. They were pulverized by German air bombardments, although foreign newspapers reported: "The Junta [Nationalist government] claims that there are no German aviators in the service of General Franco's government (140)." Don Antonio Ruiz Vilaplana, a judge in the Nationalist town of Burgos, described how the Spanish Rebel pilots felt about these air attacks: "The German aviators, reserved and serious, said nothing about the campaign, but the few Spanish airmen . . . were more talkative and were bursting with admiration. 'It's great. What material, and what fine chaps! In two hours, no more, they start out together, drop their bombs just where they want, and are back without losing their formation, and without losing a machine' (141)."

*Guernica*    The most notorious atrocity of the war was the German bombing of Guernica, a small town with a symbolic importance because of its famous oak tree. According to tradition, Spanish monarchs had stood under this tree and sworn to observe Basque rights. On 26th April, 1937, a Monday market day, Heinkels and Junkers of the Condor Legion flew over the town centre in twenty-minute raids, bombing and machine-gunning for three and a half hours. Foreign journalists visited the town that night. *The Daily Express* correspondent reported: "I walked through the still-burning town. Hundreds of bodies had been found in the debris. Most were charred beyond recognition. At least two hundred others were riddled with machine-gun bullets as they fled to the hills (142)." Eyewitness evidence was important to the Republicans because the Nationalist news-papers accused the Basques of inventing the atrocity as propa-ganda. The German air ace, Adolf Galland, later said the attack was a mistake. But a more likely reason for the bombing of Guernica was simply that the Germans wanted to observe the results of a *blitzkrieg* air attack. A Nationalist staff officer told a reporter: "We bombed it, and bombed it, and bombed it, and bueno why not? (143)" The horror of Guernica reached a world-wide audience through Picasso's monumental painting "Guern-ica" which was exhibited by the Republican government at the World's Fair in Paris.

The Basques fought desperately for national survival. Their cause was even more hopeless because their chief inland pro-vince, Navarre, had declared support for Franco. In June, their troops guarding the city of Bilbao finally gave way in the face of Nationalist battalions and German air-power. On the 19th, the town fell, and Basque freedom came to an end. The Basque language was officially forbidden, schoolmasters who were not pro-Franco were dismissed, and soon the iron mines and blast furnaces of Bilbao were working for the Rebels.

*The Basques surrender*

Some fled to the hills and continued their resistance until the fall of their last stronghold, Santander, in August. Sergeant Yolde was a Basque taken prisoner at Santander. He described the scene of panic when the city fell: "For the first time I saw a population given over to despair. People were drunk with despair and drunk with wine . . . I saw a soldier embracing his girl for the last time, and then the hand grenade he was holding in his hand exploded. I saw a ship leaving the jetty crowded with refugees . . . the ship was overloaded, but none of the passengers would get off; and the ship sailed away and sank and all were drowned (144)."

The war in the North finally ended in October when Oviedo and Gijon, the two chief towns of the other Republican enclave Asturias, surrendered under attack. The Nationalists had

91

*Overleaf* Carlist troops of the Nationalist army attack a Republican post on the outskirts of Santander

*Guernica*, Picasso's great painting of anger and protest at the brutality
of the German bombing of this Basque city

gained over 18,000 kilometres and overcome one and a half
million people. More than 60,000 Rebel soldiers were now
released to fight on other fronts.

# 5  *The Nationalist Victory*

AFTER THE WAR in the Basque country, the battlelines of 1937 remained relatively stable. Day after day, reports from the fronts read, *"Sin Novedad"* ("Nothing New"). The main offensive of the summer was a frontal attack by the Republicans against the Nationalist lines to the east of Madrid. The battle for the village of Brunete was like those of Jarama, Guadalajara and the Corunna road. Only this time, the Republican and Nationalist positions were reversed. It was the Republicans who pushed back the line a few miles without gaining a substantial breakthrough. Losses were high, particularly among the International Brigade. The XIII Brigade, composed mainly of Poles and Slavs, refused to return to the line. Their Italian commander demanded obedience at gun point.

*Battle of Brunete*

" 'No,' answered a mutineer.

" 'Think well of what you are doing,' replied the Colonel.

" 'I have.'

" 'For the last time!'

" 'No,' answered the man. The Colonel shot him dead (145)."

General Franco's overall strategy was to launch simultaneous offensives against Guadalajara and Madrid, and an eastwards thrust towards the Mediterranean. His aim was to threaten Madrid and isolate it from the province of Catalonia. The Republicans, however, seized the initiative by attacking first along the Saragossa front, particularly against the defenses of Teruel. The Battle of Teruel, fought in the worst Spanish winter for twenty years, ended the military lull and became one of the decisive battles of the war.

*Battle of Teruel*

95

A Republican army officer described the scene: "The horror was in the cold, the wind, the snow, the absence of footholds. More than half our casualties came from frostbite; many had to have their toes amputated . . . Once, many centuries ago, the fields around Teruel were probably covered with thick pine forests. Now there were men in their ice-cold pebbly trenches, keeping low to the earth, shivering, waiting for the next artillery barrage, the next burst of rifle fire, the next mortars and machine guns, and the inevitable attacks (146)."

The Republican assault on the small, bleak town of Teruel was launched on 21st December, 1937, amid a snow-storm and temperature of −20°Centigrade. Soon the Nationalist defenders retreated to their last refuge, the Seminary. A Republican officer described it: "Around the Seminary and the adjoining Santa Clara Convent there was the devil's own inferno. Green-clad, unshaven *carabineros* [Republican soldiers armed with carbines] who had been fighting fifteen days without rest, hurled bombs down into the cellars of the buildings, both of which were complete wrecks. Those below fired back with rifles (147)."

But relieving Nationalist forces were already in the outskirts of Teruel. On 31st December, two battalions, struggling through the terrible weather, made their way past the Republican lines. They recaptured the railway station and bull-ring. General Franco, in a mood of careless optimism, broadcast in his New Year message that the "brooch of Teruel" was "the clasp to the chain of the year's victories (148)."

*The Nationalists re-take the town*

But the Nationalist forces did not succeed in holding the town. On 7th January, 1938, Teruel surrendered to the Loyalist army. It was a significant but short-lived victory for the Republicans, for Franco's relieving forces were already being re-formed. The Nationalist Army of Africa, led by General Yagüe, slowly but surely surrounded Teruel and turned the Republican besiegers into the besieged. By 20th February, the Republican road and rail communications to Valencia were threatened and Loyalist forces in Teruel were facing an overwhelming offensive. A withdrawal was ordered.

*El Campesino*, the Communist military leader, was at the Battle of Teruel and was among the last to leave. He gave his

The position of the Republicans in July, 1938

special cloak to a dying comrade. It was found and given to Franco who announced on the radio, *"El Campesino* is dead." *El Campesino* heard the broadcast. He later recalled: "As soon as I had led the survivors of my command to safety, I rang up Prieto [the Minister of Defence]. *'El Campesino* speaking,' I said. 'I've broken out of Teruel with most of my men and a good deal of our material.'

" 'You're joking,' said Prieto. *'El Campesino* is dead. Who is that speaking?'

" 'Go to bloody hell,' I started, but Prieto interrupted me.

" 'Now I recognize you,' he said. 'I know you by your

Part of the crowd of 500,000 Catalans at an anti-Fascist rally in
Barcelona, addressed by Luis Companys, President of the province

vocabulary (149).' "

This act of bravado did not disguise the Republican defeat.
They had lost ten thousand dead in Teruel alone and a further
fourteen thousand had been captured. The siege and counter-
siege in Teruel showed that bravery and strategy could win a
battle, but superiority of arms and manpower would win the war.

*The
Nationalists
gain strength* The Nationalist superiority increased during 1938. Their
effective sea blockade and the closing of the border with France
sealed off the Republic from Soviet supplies. Also, the Nationalists' capture of the Basque provinces gave them much heavy
industry. In the province of Catalonia, the Anarchists were still
in power, which meant that armament production was not very
efficient. One Anarchist reported: "Notwithstanding lavish
expenditures of money on this need, our industrial organization
was not able to finish a single kind of rifle or machine gun or
cannon . . . Nonetheless it was politically necessary to sustain
at the head of the Under Secretary of Armaments an eminent
obstetrician, whose goodwill, intelligence and effort were not
sufficient to avoid industrial disaster (150)."

During a Republican offensive, a reporter asked the military
commander, General Modesto, "How many guns have they
got?"

"Eighty-four," Modesto answered.

"How many guns have we got?"

"Three."

They were guns from warships which had proclaimed their loyalty to the Republicans.

"Is that bad?"

"Yes, it's bad. They're bringing up more and more guns, and more bombers. More and more (151)."

With this superiority, particularly in planes and heavy artillery, Franco captured the port of Castellón on the Mediterranean in June. He had succeeded in cutting the Republic in two. It was now vital for the Republic to prevent more of Franco's forces from marching east. If they did, they could fan out north to Barcelona and south to Valencia.

Prime Minister Negrín responded to this threat by ordering a major Republican offensive across the Ebro River. The troops were to strike north of the newly-won Nationalist territory. Then they would wheel south and restore the link between Catalonia and the rest of Republican Spain. *The Ebro River offensive*

During the night of 24th July, 1938, the Republican attack was launched with startling suddenness along a ninety mile front. In six days, over 250 square miles were reconquered from the Nationalists. General Modesto told reporters: "We threw everything we had at them and took them by surprise. Half our men crossed the Ebro swimming, and the other half went over in Catalan fishing-boats. We used every weapon we could think of, including *chevaux de frises* [an iron ball with spikes] – a mediaeval instrument of torture specially calculated to frighten the Moors (152)."

Dizzy with the success of this long-awaited victory, Republicans dreamed of rolling Franco's forces back from the Mediterranean. Mussolini was furious: "Put on record in your diary," he told his Foreign Minister Ciano, "that today, 29th August, I prophesy the defeat of Franco . . . The Reds are fighters, Franco is not (153)."

But, as at the Battles of Brunete and Teruel, it proved easier for the Republican army to gain land than to keep it. The pattern of the Ebro campaign was the same. An immediate *A short-lived victory*

Republican success, the arrival of Nationalist reinforcements to stop the offensive, and then a successful Nationalist counter-attack. This time, however, the consequences were crucial in deciding the outcome of the whole war.

*The Nationalists' counter-offensive*

The Republican battle orders showed the commanders were desperately aware of the need for a victory: "Vigilance, fortification, and resistance." "If anyone loses an inch of ground, he must retake it at the head of his men or be executed (154)." But the Republicans were fighting with a shortage of men, rifles, machine-guns and, above all, aeroplanes. There could be only one end. Franco's counter-offensive began on 30th October, 1938. By 16th November, despite the Republican battle-order "resist, resist, resist," the last Loyalist troops had been forced back across the right-hand bank of the Ebro. Ernest Hemingway saw some of the last few survivors cross: "Naked and shivering, they made for the road and stopped a truck, from which they salvaged bits of clothes – a shirt, a coat and two pairs of ragged trousers. They were dressed in these odds and ends when they reached the remnants of the brigade (155)."

*Franco demands "unconditional surrender"*

Prime Minister Negrín realized that the Republicans had suffered a massive defeat. He put forward his first peace proposals which would have put the clock back to before 1936. They were clearly unacceptable to Franco and probably to the Anarchists and Communists as well. The proposals demanded the evacuation of foreign troops and then the holding of a national plebiscite to decide upon the structure of the state. The government which came to power would grant "regional liberties," freedom of conscience and religion, agrarian reform and an amnesty for all Spaniards. But even if Negrín's proposals had been more realistic, Franco would not have accepted them. For Franco, there would be no end to the war "other than the unconditional surrender of the vanquished to the generosity, already abundantly demonstrated, of the victors (156)." This invitation did not fool Republicans. General Miaja summed up their choice succinctly: "Either we destroy the enemy or the enemy destroys us. You can choose whether you will be the flesh that is cut up or the knife that cuts it (157)."

The only hope for the Republic was to continue to resist until

*Opposite* Neville Chamberlain, on his return from Munich, tells newsmen of his meeting with Hitler and the achievement of "peace in our time"

the Fascist aggression in Europe exploded into a world war. Then, perhaps, German and Italian aid to the Nationalists would cease, or, alternatively, Britain and France would come down off their non-intervention fence and help the Republic. Nor was this an idle hope. In September, the Spanish Nationalist Ambassador in London, the Duke of Alba, was told by the British and French governments that, in the event of a European war, Franco must declare himself neutral; otherwise he would be attacked. Franco promised neutrality, probably without much sincerity, as he expected to continue to receive aid from Germany and Italy. The Italian Foreign Minister Ciano was indignant. He knew that Franco would never aid Italy, although he expected to receive help from the Italians. "Disgusting," Ciano declared, "enough to make our dead turn in their graves (158)."

*Munich*     But Republican hopes were shattered by events which took place in Europe in the second half of 1938. In September, British Prime Minister Neville Chamberlain flew to Munich where he "solved" the Czech crisis by giving Czechoslovakia to Hitler. After this final gesture of appeasement, Stalin despaired of maintaining an effective alliance with Britain and France which would stand up to Germany. So he sought to protect the Soviet Union by befriending Hitler. This was a complete reversal of foreign policy for Stalin and as a sign of his new friendship with Germany, it was now necessary for him to withdraw the International Brigades from Spain.

*The Brigades leave Spain*     In fact, the withdrawal of the Brigades affected the Republic's morale more than its military power. By mid 1938, the majority of the Brigades' soldiers were Spanish, and the organization and expertise of the volunteers had been copied successfully by the rest of the Republican army. The farewell parade was held in Barcelona on 15th November. *La Pasionaria* outdid herself at this tear-jerking occasion: "Comrades of the International Brigades! Political reasons, reasons of State, the welfare of that same cause for which you offered your blood with boundless generosity, are sending you back, some of you to your own countries and others to forced exile. You can go proudly. You are history. You are legend. You are the heroic example of

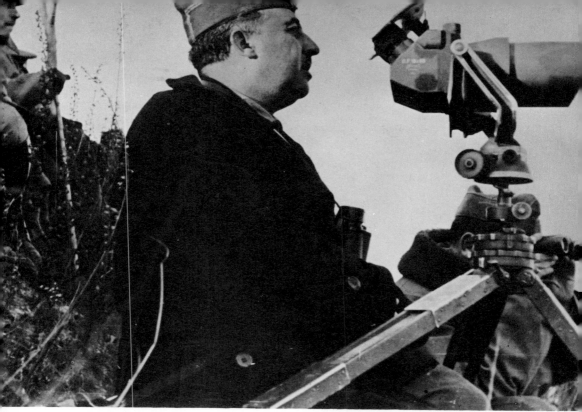

General Franco watches his troops advance towards Barcelona, in a
massive onslaught on Republican territory

democracy's solidarity and universality. We shall not forget you,
and when the olive tree of peace puts forth its leaves again,
mingled with the laurels of the Spanish Republic's victory –
come back!! (159)"

Another reason for the fall in the Republicans' morale was the *Low food* chronic shortage of food in the areas they held. As propaganda, *supplies* the Nationalists dropped loaves of bread from aeroplanes over Madrid and Barcelona. The Republicans replied by dropping packages of shirts and socks in Nationalist areas to demonstrate their manufacturing superiority. In Madrid, which the Republicans still held, there was no coal, no gas and little electricity; the *Madrileños* lived on handfuls of lentils and less than two ounces of bread per person per day; only babies could receive milk. The average rations of the Republican troops had shrunk steadily (160):

103

Republican machine-gunners try to stem the Nationalist advance on Barcelona

|              | *1936*    | *1937*    | *1938*    |
| ------------ | --------- | --------- | --------- |
| *Bread*      | 700 grams | 600 grams | 400 grams |
| *Meat or Fish* | 250 grams | 200 grams | 150 grams |

Ricardo del Rio, a wartime director of the Republican news agency, Febus, wrote afterwards: "In Catalonia, where people had been particularly accustomed to living well throughout the war, not even five per cent were willing to undergo the short rations demanded of them by the [Republican] government (161)."

After its withdrawal across the Ebro River, the Republican army became desperate for material, and its morale sank. Seventy thousand troops were dead, wounded or captured, and 200 aircraft, 1,800 machine-guns and 24,000 rifles were lost. The army was no longer a fighting force capable of resisting the Nationalist troops in North Spain. Franco's army, strengthened by a fresh detachment of German soldiers to the Condor Legion, advanced through Catalonia. They met scarcely any resistance.

The constant siege of Madrid by Nationalist troops had stiffened the *Madrileños'* fighting spirit. The same could not be said of the Catalans when Franco's armies approached Barcelona. In the words of Colonel Vicente Rojo, the Republican Chief of Staff: "Barcelona was a city of the dead. The cause of death was demoralization, caused by both those who fled . . . and those who stayed in hiding. It is no exaggeration to assert that there was no will to resist either in the civilian population or in some of the troops who had become contaminated by the atmosphere. Morale was at rock bottom (162)."

A group of women give an enthusiastic reception for Franco's troops as they enter Barcelona

*Overleaf* Thousands of Spanish refugees and Republican militia fled across the frontier to France as the Nationalists advanced into Catalonia

Barcelona, the city of Durruti's triumph and Orwell's dreams, was taken with very little trouble on 26th January, 1939. One eyewitness reported: "Soldiers . . . threw down their guns as soon as the first enemy forces approached (163)." Dr. Marcel Junod of the International Red Cross was there. He later described the scene as the Nationalist troops arrived: "At half past one, the first tank roared down the street and came to a halt before our quarters. The crew consisted of German soldiers. Perched on top of the tank was a smiling woman giving the Fascist salute to the crowd . . . During the afternoon red and gold monarchist flags began to appear on balconies of Barcelona . . . An endless column of *Requetés* in red berets, Falangists, and Moors with their patient mules moved slowly down towards the town. By evening Barcelona was completely occupied (164)."

Terrified of the victors' revenge, the vanquished fled north across the Pyrenees; about half a million Catalan refugees made

A tragic refugee from the advancing Nationalists is helped on her way

their way into France and thrust themselves on the French government's mercy. Prime Minister Negrín and his government, the Communist leaders, the chiefs of the army and civil service, together with the Catalan and *emigré* Basque governments, moved to Gerona, which was near the French border. Here they set up their final headquarters.

On 1st February, 1939, the survivors of the *Cortes*, elected with such enthusiasm three years before, held their final meeting in the dungeon of Figueras Castle, the last Catalan town before the French border. Herbert Matthews, the *New York Times* reporter, witnessed the ceremony: "It was in this setting, with the Republican flag displayed for the last time at a Cortes of the Second Republic, with its tribune covered with red brocade, with cheap carpets on the stone floor and plain wooden seats, that Martinez Barrio tapped his gavel at 10.25 on the night of 1st February, 1939, and the session began (165)." Negrín then proposed a three point peace offer: a guarantee of Spanish independence, a guarantee that Spaniards could choose their own government, a guarantee that no Spaniard would suffer persecution for his part in the war. If these were not granted, Negrín declared, "We will continue to fight in the central zone. Countries do not live only by victories, but by the examples which their people have known how to give in tragic times." It was on that noble theme that the long speech ended. "No one could call it an oratorical masterpiece; it was disjointed, and badly delivered, by a man so exhausted that he could hardly stand, yet it should take its place with the great documents of Spanish history (166)."

*Last meeting of the Cortes*

After the *Cortes* had been dissolved, most of its members fled to France where they joined Aguirre (ex-President of the Basque Republic), Companys (ex-President of Catalonia), Caballero (ex-Socialist Prime Minister of Republican Spain), and Azaña (ex-President of Republican Spain). Azaña's inglorious departure from Spain had contradicted the brave words he had spoken after his election in 1936: "To defend the Republic, if need be, I will shed the last drop of my blood (167)." Yet his abrupt escape made little difference to the government he left behind. Azaña had never succeeded in bolstering Republican morale.

*Government members flee*

A Republican wrote later: "The extent of his influence during the war, both at home and abroad, was shown by his extinction. He never succeeded in making his authority felt and . . . his activity was limited to the delivery of two or three speeches (168)."

Azaña's escape was shameful yet his reasons for deserting were realistic. He explained: "I refuse to help, by my presence, to prolong a senseless struggle . . . Nobody believes in our powers of resistance and the most sceptical of all are our own generals (169)."

Prime Minister Negrín's position was indeed hopeless. On 18th February, 1939, Franco declared: "The Nationalists have won. The Republicans must therefore surrender without conditions (170)." On 27th February, Britain and France recognized Franco; in the House of Commons the Labour leader, Major Clement Attlee, accused Chamberlain of "a gross betrayal of democracy, the consummation of two and half years of the hypocritical pretence of non-intervention and a connivance all the time at aggression (171)."

*Negrín continues the fight*

But Negrín realized that if he accepted Franco's invitation to "surrender without conditions," the Republicans could expect dreadful reprisals. By continuing the fight he had little to lose and, as a close colleague said, "We thought that the only way of obtaining any . . . act of grace from General Franco was by combining such pressure as might be applied on the international plane with an attitude that gave the impression we were prepared to go on fighting (172)."

Negrín's leadership was still backed by some real power. Madrid, Valencia and about one quarter of Spain were still in Republican hands; the Communists pledged support to the Republic and iron resistance against the Fascists.

*The army revolts*

Yet the War ended only one month later. On 5th March the Republican General Miaja and his deputy Colonel Casado led an army revolt in Madrid against the government. They appointed a Defence Council which consisted of the main Popular Front parties with the exception of the Communists. Negrín phoned Miaja from Valencia:

"What is going on in Madrid, General?" he asked.

"What is going on is that I have revolted," Casado replied.

"That you have revolted! Against whom? Against me?"

"Yes, against you!"

"Very well, you can consider yourself relieved of your command! (173)"

But it was too late. Negrín was overthrown and flew to France within twenty-four hours. The army had revolted because they felt defeat was inevitable. In Madrid alone, four to five hundred people were dying of starvation every week. Some influential citizens believed it was possible for them to make an advantageous treaty with Franco. Many others were turning against the Communists now that the hope of victory had disappeared. So the War ended the same way it began: a revolt by a minority of the Republican army against the Republican government. *The war ends as it began*

Now the final tragedy was played out in the streets of Madrid as Communists and Republicans turned on one another. An eyewitness wrote: "For many days, men who had stood shoulder to shoulder resisting Franco fired upon one another. The few remaining Loyalist planes dropped bombs on Loyalists. The streets of Madrid, which no Rebel had trod, ran with Republican blood . . . It was a miserable close for a saga of national heroism (174)." *Blood-stained streets*

With his enemies fighting each other, General Franco bided his time, as did the vanguard of his troops who had held out in the University City in Madrid for twenty-seven months. By 12th March, the Communists, who had pledged resistance against the Fascists, had been squashed. By 27th March, the Republican air force had surrendered, many infantry units had deserted and the Defence Council set up by General Miaja had fled. On 28th March, 200,000 Nationalist troops peacefully entered Madrid. Now the "Fifth Column" of Nationalist sympathizers appeared. *The Times* correspondent commented on these sympathizers who had concealed themselves during the War: "One noticed among the crowds a few 'whites' who had lain in hiding, dazed, pallid, corpselike, some of them out in the daylight for the first time for thirty-two months. Many people looked surprisingly well dressed. No one who owned and had been able to conceal smart clothes had dared to wear them . . . The lavish use of lipstick and cosmetics among young women *The "Fifth Column" appears*

111

of all classes . . . doubtless hid much pallor (175)."

The capitulation of Madrid marked the end of the War. White flags were hoisted in the cities of Cordoba and Toledo. On 1st April, this communiqué was issued (176):

"Today, after capturing and disarming the Red Army, the National troops have attained their last military objectives.

"The war is over.

GENERALISSIMO FRANCO

BURGOS 1st APRIL 1939
YEAR OF VICTORY"

# Conclusion

THE SPANISH CIVIL WAR lasted for two years and 254 days, and resulted in a complete victory for General Franco.

The cost was enormous. About 500,000 people were killed in action, died of disease, or were executed; after the war, tens of thousands of Republicans were shot, over 250,000 were imprisoned for up to thirty years and 340,000 others chose exile. More than 250,000 houses were destroyed and over 150 whole towns severely damaged. Spain lost one-third of her livestock and, when the war ended, supplies of raw materials and food were desperately low. The Nationalists estimated that the war cost £3,000 million or $7,500 million in 1938 values. They refused to recognize any money issued by the Republican government after 18th July, 1936, so many Republicans went bankrupt.

*Cost of the war*

General Franco lost no time in moving his administration from Burgos to Madrid. He has ruled as a right-wing dictator ever since. There is now only one legal political party – the National Movement – which incorporates the Falange. Freedom of speech is limited. The Church has now become more independent and is even considering making a public apology for its role in the Civil War. But the army is still Franco's main power and protection. A Spanish journalist said recently: "Of course, you realize all our tanks are facing inwards towards our cities, not outwards towards our borders (177)."

*Franco in power*

In April, 1939, an English journalist, Karl Robson, took shelter just north of the Spanish frontier. He wrote: "The Spanish war is over. But Europe is astir, and armies are on the alert. As I see in my mind's eye the destroyed towns and villages

*A world war?*

113

Reprisals for resistance: the cost in human life was enormous, the cost
to Spain herself immeasurable

of Spain, the roasted bodies, the dead, drained faces lolling
from mules . . . I wonder whether such tragic scenes are shortly
to be re-enacted on a larger and more crowded stage. If the
nationalist megalomaniacs of Europe had a few similar memories
fresh in their minds, I should not, perhaps, be asking in the peace
of St. Jean de Luz, 'Where next?' (178)" One of Franco's
achievements was to keep Spain out of the Second World War
which began six months later. The outbreak of the war, however,
prevented Spain from receiving badly needed aid.

*Hitler's*
*intervention*

What effect did the intervention of these "nationalist megalomaniacs" have on the outcome of the Civil War? Probably the
crucial period was the autumn of 1938. After Munich Stalin
lost interest in Spain. Hitler realized he could get away with
anything. His huge injection of arms and manpower into the
Condor Legion revived the Nationalist army and led to its
successful campaign against Catalonia. This was the beginning

of the end.

Franco's main achievement during the War was to unite the disparate elements in Nationalist Spain – the Falange, Church, Monarchists and Army; this unity was effective because each party in Franco's alliance believed that no political aim was so important as victory. The Republic fell because of its disunity, which arose from the Republicans' assumption that political ideals were more important than defeat.

The Anarchists were prepared to destroy the Republican system, but not prepared to make the political and military compromises that war demands. The Socialists also failed to resolve the conflict between ideology and reality. A Spanish historian summed up how the left-wing parties undermined the Popular Front: "The obstacles presented, for supposedly ideological reasons, to the building of a genuine and efficient army; the disorientation in industrial and agrarian work; the scandalous incapacity of many Republican and labour leaders; the depressing spectacle of the disagreements and clashes, sometimes bloody, between the parties and labour groups that were fighting against Franco . . . (179)"

*The Left fails to unite*

Only the Communists were able to provide the leadership, discipline and military backing needed to win. But they depended on Russia's fickle foreign policy and they never won popularity in Spain, despite their election successes. In fact, to many Spaniards, even to those who nominally supported the Republic, it was Franco's Spain which was truly "nationalist" or "Spanish." When the chips were down, many Spanish Catholics showed greater determination and self-sacrifice than the Anarchists in Catalonia.

The official secondary-school history syllabus of 1939 shows how Franco built on the Spaniards' pride in their nation, although the facts were distorted. The students were expected to learn how "freemasonry and international Jewish finance causes the fall of the monarchy. The Second Republic. Its anti-national and anti-Catholic propaganda. Its disasters, disorders and crimes . . . Bolshevik and Marxist invasions.

"The National Movement. Its historical justification . . . Franco. Spain recovers her historic personality (180)."

# Table of Events

**1936**

| | |
|---|---|
| 16th February | General elections. Victory of Popular Front. |
| 17th–18th July | The Generals launch the uprising. |
| 19th July | President Giral asks France for help. Generals Mola and Sanjurjo ask Italy. |
| 23rd July | Inauguration of Committee of National Defence in Burgos. |
| 4th September | Largo Caballero becomes Prime Minister. |
| 9th September | First meeting of Non-Intervention Committee. |
| 1st October | Franco declared "Chief of Spanish State." |
| 22nd–25th October | Transfer of Republic's gold reserves to Soviet Union. |
| 7th–8th November | International Brigade reaches Madrid; Battle of Madrid begins. |
| 20th November | Execution of José Antonio Primo de Rivera. |
| 23rd November | End of battle for University of Madrid. |
| 30th November | Death of Buenaventura Durruti. |

**1937**

| | |
|---|---|
| 15th January | End of second phase in Battle of Madrid. |
| 8th February | Fall of Malaga. |
| 11th–28th February | Battle of Jarama. |
| 8th–13th March | Rout of Italians at Guadalajara. |
| 26th April | Germans bomb Guernica. |
| 17th May | Caballero's government falls. Dr. Juan Negrín becomes Prime Minister. |

| | |
|---|---|
| 6th–26th July | Battle of Brunete. |
| 21st October | Gijon falls; Nationalists victorious in the North. |
| 15th December | Republican troops attack Teruel. |

## 1938

| | |
|---|---|
| 7th January | Teruel surrenders to Republican troops. |
| 21st February | Rebels retake Teruel. |
| 9th March | Rebels begin Aragón offensive. |
| 17th June | Rebels take Castellón on Mediterranean. |
| 24th–25th July | Colonel Modesto begins Ebro offensive. |
| 22nd September | International Brigades withdrawn from fronts. |
| 30th September | Munich Agreement between Hitler and Chamberlain. |
| 4th October | Negrín broadcasts peace plans. |
| 16th November | Republican troops forced back across the Ebro. |
| 23rd December | Franco opens offensive on Catalonia. |

## 1939

| | |
|---|---|
| 26th January | Barcelona falls. |
| 1st February | Last meeting of *Cortes* at Figueras. |
| 5th February | Republican leaders leave Spain. |
| 18th February | Franco declares victory. |
| 27th February | Britain and France recognize Franco's claim. |
| 5th March | Army revolt in Madrid; Negrín flees. |
| 28th March | Madrid falls. |
| 29th March | Hostilities cease. |
| 1st April | Franco's victory communiqué; U.S.A. recognizes Franco. |

# Dramatis Personae

ALFONSO XIII (1886–1941) Last Bourbon King of Spain. His grandson, Juan Carlos, has been named by Franco as his successor.

AGUIRRE, JOSÉ (1904–60) President of the Basque Republic.

AZAÑA, MANUEL (1880–1940) Prime Minister of the Spanish Republic (1931–33, 1936, and President, 1936–39.)

COMPANYS, LUIS (1883–1940) President of Catalonia.

DURRUTI, BUENAVENTURA (1896–1936) A leading Anarchist.

FRANCO, General FRANCISCO (1892–    ) Commander in the Canaries, Nationalist Generalissimo and now *Caudillo* (head of state) of Spain.

HEMINGWAY, ERNEST (1899–1961) American novelist whose support for the Republic is evident in his novel of the Civil War, *For Whom the Bell Tolls*.

KOESTLER, ARTHUR (1905–    ) Hungarian, Communist journalist working for the Republic.

LARGO CABALLERO, FRANCISCO (1869–1946) President of Spanish Socialist Party and U.G.T. Minister of Labour 1931–33, and Prime Minister of the Republic 1936–37.

MARTY, ANDRÉ (1886–1956) Frenchman; Commander of the International Brigades.

MUSSOLINI, BENITO (1883–1945) Founder and *Duce* (leader) of Italian Fascism, which influenced Nazis and Falange.

NEGRÍN, Dr. JUAN (1889–1956) Socialist Prime Minister of the Republic 1937–39; relied heavily on Communists.

ORWELL, GEORGE (1903–50) Real name Eric Blair; English writer – *Homage to Catalonia* – who fought for P.O.U.M. militia.

LA PASIONARIA (1895–     ) Real name Dolores Ibarruri; a Spanish Communist leader and now the leader of exiled Spanish Communist Party.

ROBLES, GIL (1898–     ) Leader of C.E.D.A. (the Conservative Catholic Party).

PRIMO de RIVERA, JOSÉ ANTONIO (1903–36) Founder and leader of the Falange.

QUEIPO de LLANO, General GONZALO (1875–1951) Nationalist general.

STALIN, JOSEF (1879–1953) Real name Josef Dzhugashvili; Communist dictator of the Soviet Union. Stalin's outlook was nationalistic. His main concern was to transform the Soviet Union into a Socialist and then a Communist state.

# Glossary

ANARCHISM. A philosophical belief that all government is bad, and people should form voluntary groups.

ANARCHISTS. The Spanish revolutionary "people's party." (see C.N.T. and F.I.A.)

CARLISTS. A para-military organization which, like the Monarchists, fought for the return of the monarchy; but, while the Monarchists supported the Bourbon line, the Carlists backed the descendants of the nineteenth century claimant, Don Carlos.

C.N.T. (*Confederación Nacional de Trabajo*). The Anarchists' Trade Union.

COMMUNISM. Ideally, a political movement guided by the principle: "From each according to his ability, to each according to his needs." Should the principle ever be achieved, class distinctions, property, and the State itself would disappear. Communism is preceded by Socialism, where the State takes over the means of production (industry, agriculture, commerce) in order to increase its power and redistribute wealth in accordance with social justice.

F.I.A. (*Federación Anarquista Ibérica*.) The Anarchist secret society and terrorist organization.

FALANGE. Spain's semi-Fascist movement.

FASCISM. A nationalist, anti-Communist movement. A Fascist state is ruled by a single-party dictatorship which extends its power over private and public life and uses the media for propaganda purposes.

P.O.U.M. (*Partido Obrero de Unificación Marxista*.) Spanish

120

Trotskyists, i.e. supporters of Russian Leon Trotsky who advocated international, at the expense of national, Communism.

U.G.T. (*Unión General de Trabajadores.*) The Socialist Trade Union.

# Further Reading

Hugh Thomas, *The Spanish Civil War* (Penguin, 1971; Harper-Row, 1961). This is generally considered the fairest and most comprehensive history of the Spanish Civil War in English.

Robert Payne, *The Civil War in Spain* (Secker & Warburg, 1962; Putnam, 1970). One of the "History in the Making" series which tells the story through eyewitness accounts.

Stanley G. Payne, *The Spanish Revolution* (Weidenfeld & Nicolson, 1970; Norton, 1970). Concentrates on Spanish politics during this period.

Stanley Weintraub, *The Last Great Cause* (W. H. Allen, 1968; Weybright, 1968). A study of the involvement of English and American writers in the war.

The three best known books by foreign writers who went to Spain (they all supported the Republic) are:

Ernest Hemingway, *For Whom the Bell Tolls* (Penguin, 1969; Scribner, 1940). For Hemingway, this novel represented "everything I had learned about Spain for eighteen years."

George Orwell, *Homage to Catalonia* (Penguin, 1962; Harcourt Brace, 1969). This is Orwell's account of his experiences in the war and of the political squabbling in Catalonia.

Arthur Koestler, *Spanish Testimony* (Gollancz, 1937). This book includes "Dialogue with Death," Koestler's account of life in a Nationalist condemned cell. At times, journalistic objectivity clashes with propaganda; because of this, Koestler has refused republication after the first printing.

# Notes on Sources

(1) Tom Wintringham, *Inside Fascist Spain* (London, 1943)
(2) Captain Liddell Hart, quoted in *Ibid*
(3) Arthur Koestler, quoted in Stanley Weintraub, *The Last Great Cause* (London, 1968)
(4) Quoted in *Ibid*
(5) Ernest Hemingway, *For Whom the Bell Tolls* (Penguin, 1969)
(6) Georges Bernanos; quoted in Hugh Thomas, *The Spanish Civil War* (London, 1971)
(7) Quoted by Theo Aronson in *Royal Vendetta* (London, 1966)
(8) Giménez Caballero; quoted in Thomas, *op cit.*
(9) Quoted in *Ibid*
(10) Stanley Payne, *The Spanish Revolution* (London, 1970)
(11) Quoted in Thomas, *op cit*
(12) *Ibid*
(13) *Ibid*
(14) Quoted in Robert Payne, *The Civil War in Spain* (London, 1963)
(15) *Ibid*
(16) Frank Jellinek, *The Civil War in Spain* (London, 1938)
(17) Arthur Koestler, *Spanish Testimony* (London, 1937)
(18) Quoted in Thomas,
(19) Quoted in Koestler, *op. cit.*
(20) Quoted in Thomas, *op. cit.*
(21) Jellinek, *op. cit.*
(22) *Ibid*
(23) Quoted in Thomas, *op. cit.*
(24) Jellinek, *op. cit.*
(25) Koestler, *op. cit.*
(26) Quoted in Stanley Payne, *op. cit.*
(27) Quoted in Jellinek, *op. cit.*
(28) *Ibid*
(29) Quoted in Koestler, *op. cit.*
(30) Jellinek, *op. cit.*
(31) Stanley Payne, *op. cit.*
(32) Quoted in Koestler, *op. cit.*
(33) *Ibid*
(34) Miguel Maura; quoted in Stanley Payne, *op. cit.*
(35) Julián Besteiro; quoted in Stanley Payne, *op. cit.*
(36) Quoted in Robert Payne, *op. cit.*
(37) *Ibid*
(38) Told by Gerrold and quoted in Weintraub, *op. cit.*
(39) From diary of Constancia de la Mora; quoted in Robert Payne, *op. cit.*
(40) *Ibid*
(41) Quoted in Robert Payne, *op. cit.*
(42) By now, Spanish legend
(43) Arturo Barea, *The Clash* (London, 1946)
(44) Told by Colonel Moscardo and quoted in Thomas, *op. cit.*
(45) Koestler, *op. cit.*
(46) Quoted in *Ibid*
(47) *Ibid*
(48) *Ibid*
(49) Quoted in Thomas, *op. cit.*
(50) Koestler, *op. cit.*
(51) Karl Robson, essay in *Foreign Correspondent* (London, 1939)
(52) Quoted in Koestler, *op. cit.*
(53) E. L. Taylor; quoted *Ibid*
(54) Quoted in Thomas, *Ibid*
(55) *Ibid*
(56) From memorandum published by Madrid University and quoted in Koestler, *op. cit.*
(57) Quoted *Ibid*
(58) A. Hitler, *Mein Kampf* (London, 1969)
(59) Quoted in Koestler, *op. cit.*
(60) Quoted in Weintraub, *op. cit.*
(61) Claud Cockburn (pseudonym Frank Pitcairn), *Reporter in Spain* (London, 1936)
(62) Told by Christopher Caudwell and quoted in Weintraub, *op. cit.*
(63) George Orwell, *Homage to Catalonia* (London, 1938)
(64) Quoted in Thomas, *op. cit.*
(65) *Ibid*
(66) Orwell, *op. cit.*

(67) H. E. Kaminski; quoted in Thomas, *op. cit.*

(68) García Oliver; quoted *Ibid*

(69) Quoted *Ibid*

(70) W. Horsfall Carter, "Spain Today," *The Listener* (May, 1936)

(71) Quoted in Stanley Payne, *op. cit.*

(72) Diego Abad de Santillán (leader of F.I.A.); quoted in Thomas, *op. cit.*

(73) Federica Montseny; quoted *Ibid*

(74) Orwell, *op. cit.*

(75) Quoted in Thomas, *op. cit.*

(76) *Ibid*

(77) Dante Puzzo, "The Non-Intervention Committee and Italo-German Aid to the Nationalists;" *Problems in European Civilization* (Boston, 1967)

(78) Quoted in Jellinek, *op. cit.*

(79) Dante Puzzo, *op. cit.*

(80) Jellinek, *op. cit.*

(81) Quoted in Thomas, *op. cit.*

(82) Dante Puzzo, *op. cit.*

(83) *Ibid*

(84) *Ibid*

(85) *Ibid*

(86) Quoted in Thomas, *op. cit.*

(87) *Poems for Spain* (Hogarth Press, London, 1939)

(88) *Nuremberg Trials. LX*

(89) Quoted in Thomas, *op. cit.*

(90) Koestler, *op. cit.*

(91) Quoted in Thomas, *op. cit.*

(92) Hitler, *op. cit.*

(93) G. T. Garratt, *Mussolini's Roman Empire* (London, 1938)

(94) Quoted in Thomas, *op. cit.*

(95) Ernest Hambloch, *Italy Militant* (London, 1941)

(96) Quoted in Garratt, *op. cit.*

(97) *Ibid*

(98) *Ibid*

(99) David T. Cattell, "Soviet Military Aid to the Republic," *Problems in European Civilization* (Boston, 1967)

(100) *Ibid*

(101) *Ibid*

(102) Quoted in Thomas, *op. cit.*

(103) Quoted in Stanley Payne, *op. cit.*

(104) *Ibid*

(105) *Ibid*

(106) *Ibid*

(107) Quoted in Thomas, *op. cit.*

(108) *Ibid*

(109) *Ibid*

(110) Ralph Fox; quoted in Weintraub, *op. cit.*

(111) Tom Wintringham, *English Captain* (London, 1939)

(112) *Poems for Spain*

(113) Quoted in Weintraub, *op. cit.*

(114) Orwell, *op. cit.*

(115) Quoted in Robert Payne, *op. cit.*

(116) Hemingway, *op. cit.*

(117) Quoted in Weintraub, *op. cit.*

(118) Quoted in Thomas, *op. cit.*

(119) Noel Monks; quoted in *Ibid*

(120) Arturo Barea, *op. cit.*

(121) Quoted in Robert Payne, *op. cit.*

(122) Thomas, *op. cit.*

(123) *Ibid*

(124) Quoted Weintraub, *op. cit.*

(125) Esmond Romilly, *Boadilla* (London, 1937)

(126) *Poems for Spain*

(127) Orwell, *op. cit.*

(128) *Ibid*

(129) *Ibid*

(130) Koestler, *op. cit.*

(131) Quoted in Robert Payne, *op. cit.*

(132) *Poems for Spain*

(133) Quoted in Weintraub, *op. cit.*

(134) *Ibid*

(135) Quoted in Robert Payne, *op. cit.*

(136) *Ibid*

(137) Quoted in Garratt, *op. cit.*

(138) Quoted in Weintraub, *op. cit.*

(139) Garratt *op. cit.*

(140) *Morning Post.* April, 1937

(141) Quoted in Garratt, *op. cit.*

(142) Noel Monks of the *Daily Express*, April, 1937

(143) Quoted in Thomas, *op. cit.*

(144) Quoted in Robert Payne, *op. cit.*

(145) Quoted in Thomas, *op. cit.*

(146) Quoted in Robert Payne, *op. cit.*

(147) Henry Buckley; quoted *Ibid*

(148) E. Allison Peers,

*Spain in Eclipse:*
1937 –43 (London, 1943)

(149) Quoted in Robert Payne, *op. cit.*

(150) Colonel Vicente Rojo; quoted in Stanley Payne, *op. cit.*

(151) Quoted in Robert Payne, *op. cit.*

(152) *Ibid*

(153) Ciano, *Diary*, 1937–38 (London, 1952)

(154) Quoted in Thomas, *op. cit.*

(155) Quoted in Weintraub, *op. cit.*

(156) Quoted in Peers, *op. cit.*

(157) *Ibid*

(158) Ciano, *op. cit.*

(159) Quoted in Thomas, *op. cit.*

(160) Quoted in Stanley Payne, *op. cit.*

(161) *Ibid*

(162) *Ibid*

(163) Quoted in Robert Payne, *op. cit.*

(164) *Ibid*

(165) *Ibid*

(166) Quoted in Peers, *op. cit.*

(167) Colonel Rojo; quoted *Ibid*

(168) Quoted *Ibid*

(169) *Ibid*

(170) Quoted Thomas, *op. cit.*

(171) Alvarez del Vayo; quoted *Ibid*

(172) Álvarez del Vayo; quoted in Robert Payne, *op. cit.*

(173) Louis Fischer, *Men and Politics* (London, 1941)

(174) A. James, "Madrid After the Fall," *The Times*, April, 1939

(175) Quoted in Peers, *op. cit.*

(176) *Ibid*

(177) *The New Statesman*, August, 1972

(178) Karl Robson, *op. cit.*

(179) Anton Rovira; quoted in Stanley Payne, *op. cit.*

(180) Quoted in Peers, *op. cit.*

# Picture Credits

The author and publishers wish to thank all those who have given permission for copyright illustrations to appear on the following pages: Musée de l'Art Moderne, Paris, jacket; Keystone, *frontispiece*, 10, 18, 26, 29, 32, 36, 39, 41, 58, 61, 63, 67, 73, 74, 78, 80, 82, 103, 104, 105, 106–107, 114; Radio Times Hulton Picture Library, 15, 19, 21, 49, 57, 108; Paul Popper 30, 50, 53, 79, 85, 92–93, 98, 101; B.B.C., 35; Camera Press, 46; Pablo Picasso and S.P.A.D.E.M., 94. The maps on pages 24 and 98 are reproduced from *The Spanish Civil War* by Hugh Thomas by the kind permission of the publishers, Eyre and Spotiswoode. That on page 34 is reproduced from Martin Gilbert's *Recent History Atlas* by the kind permission of Weidenfeld & Nicolson and Crowell-Collier Macmillan.

# Acknowledgements

The Publishers wish to thank the Hogarth Press for permission to quote from Edgell Rickword's poem, "To the wife of any non-intervention statesman" and from John Lepper's "Battle of Jarama 1937," both of which were published in *Poems for Spain* (1939) and for permission to quote an extract from Sir Herbert Read's poem, "A song for the Spanish Anarchists," which was published in *Thirty-Five Poems* (1940). The Publishers also wish to thank Faber & Faber for permission to quote from Stephen Spender's poem, "Ultima ration regum," which appeared in his *Collected Poems 1928–53* (1953). Acknowledgements are also due to the Executors of the Estate of C. Day-Lewis, Jonathan Cape Ltd., the Hogarth Press and Harold Matson Co., Inc., for permission to quote from "The Nabara," which appeared in C. Day-Lewis's *Collected Poems* (1954) and to the Executors of the John Cornford Estate, Jonathan Cape Ltd., and the editor, Pat Sloan, for permission to quote from "Full moon at Tierz" by John Cornford which was published in *A Memoir*.

# Index